Manju Ma.... has .. ..pproach to cooking Indian food at home, with presenting TV shows in Asia as well as the UK. Manju grew up surrounded by Indian culture and traditions and several years of her childhood were spent in ... .pice runs through her veins and she is aware of many of ...aluable properties and benefits which can play an ...tant role in good and healthy living. Manju lives in London ...e she teaches people of all ages, from 8 to 80, how to cook ...ily, and in return they laugh at her jokes. She was recently ...nised in the Queen's Honours List for her charity work and ...ded the BEM.

...r recent books include *Everyday Healthy Indian Cookery*, *...Indian Cookbook* and *Classic Indian Recipes*.

The Seasoned Foodie

Nutritious Dishes for a Healthier, Longer Life

Manju Malhi

....

A HOW TO BOOK

ROBINSON

ROBINSON

First published in Great Britain in 2021 by Robinson

10 9 8 7 6 5 4 3 2 1

Copyright © Manju Malhi, 2021

A CIP catalogue record for this book is available from the British Library.

ISBN: 978-1-47214-584-0

Typeset by Basement Press, Glaisdale
Printed and bound in Great Britain by Clays Ltd, Elcograf S.p.A.

Papers used by Robinson are from well-managed forests and other responsible sources.

MIX
Paper from
responsible sources
FSC® C104740

Robinson
An imprint of
Little, Brown Book Group
Carmelite House
50 Victoria Embankment
London EC4Y 0DZ

An Hachette UK Company
www.hachette.co.uk

www.littlebrown.co.uk

How To Books are published by Robinson, an imprint of Little, Brown Book Group. We welcome proposals from authors who have first-hand experience of their subjects. Please set out the aims of your book, its target market and its suggested contents in an email to howtobooks@littlebrown.co.uk

To my mum Kami who epitomises the ethos of Open Age

Contents

Introduction

Whatever your age, maintaining an active lifestyle and eating a balanced diet is an important part of supporting good health. It also reduces your risk of disease, infection and other illnesses. Above all, it can help you feel your best.

As we get older, many of us eat less because our energy output generally reduces with age and our appetite is likely to shrink. However, our desire to eat doesn't lessen. Even if we have a smaller appetite and require fewer calories, our body still needs vitamins, minerals and nutrients to sustain us. *The Seasoned Foodie* is the definitive guide to satisfying both your dietary needs and your love of good food with maximum nutrition and flavour, while requiring minimum effort.

According to the World Health Organisation (WHO), the majority of diseases that people over the age of 60 suffer from are a result of poor diet. For example, the consumption of high-fat foods has been linked to certain cancers of the prostate, colon and pancreas. Poor diet also plays a significant role in a number of deficiency diseases, including diabetes and osteoporosis. A deficiency of micronutrients – such as vitamins A, D and E, and zinc, calcium and iron – is a common problem and often it arises because there's a lack of diversity in our diet.

As we grow older our taste buds change, which correlates with changes in our food cravings. We also experience changes that affect the ability to detect flavour. This is often accompanied and impacted by a reduced sense of smell, as fewer nerve endings in the nose can dull the ability to smell and taste. The production of saliva too is diminished, which can affect our overall appetite as well as our food choices. Some of us may find it difficult to eat healthily and stay hydrated because of underlying health conditions or mobility challenges.

From the age of around 45 years old, we tend to start losing 1 per cent of our muscle mass year by year. This gradual reduction of strength leads to the onset of frailty. This weakness can in turn lead to a higher frequency of falls and fractures, the hip fracture being the most common. One way of avoiding this is to eat plenty of protein. A high protein intake of about 90g per day is suitable for a person weighing 70kg (about 11 stone), in combination with remaining active. Weight-bearing exercises can help strengthen legs, and resistance exercises utilising weights can be used to stress the muscles in a good way. Always check with your doctor before embarking on any different form of exercise or eating habit.

Life expectancy in the UK has doubled over the last two hundred years, and now around 16 per cent (approximately 10 million) of the population is aged over 65. Within the older age group, there has been a massive increase in the number of people aged 85 years and over. Unfortunately, these extra years added to our lifespan are not necessarily 'healthy', and this has a detrimental impact on the quality of life of older people.

Older people are at an increased risk of heart disease and Type 2 diabetes if their waist circumference is:

- Men – over 94cm (substantially increased risk over 102cm)
- Women – over 80cm (substantially increased risk over 88cm)

WHEN TO EAT

We're often told that weight gain and diseases such as heart disease and Type 2 diabetes are connected with the simple matter of the quantity and type of food we consume, balanced with the number of calories we expend through exercise, but mounting evidence suggests that timing is also important. It's not just what you eat, but when you eat that matters.

The idea that our metabolic response to food varies at different times of day dates back to the studies of ancient Chinese medics.

They believed that energy flowed around the body in parallel with the sun's movements, and that our meals should be timed accordingly. 7am to 9am was the 'time of the stomach', when the biggest meal of the day should be consumed. Evening dinner or supper they believed should be a light affair, consumed between 5pm and 7pm, which was when kidney function predominated.

Eating meals at the right time of the day can provide many benefits that help you maintain a healthy weight, keep your energy up and perhaps even help fight off disease.

Breakfast

Breakfast is widely recognised as the most important meal of the day, partly because it sets the pattern for your blood sugar for the rest of the day, so it is recommended to refrain from consuming sweet pastries or sugary coffee beverages. It is advised to eat within the first hour you wake up, between the hours of 6am and 10am. Eating healthy fats present in fish and seeds; whole grains like oats, barley and buckwheat or wholegrain cereals; and protein in foods such as plain yogurt, eggs or cottage cheese are a few healthy suggestions.

Lunch

Your body has a stronger digestive function between 10am and 2pm, which makes it an ideal time to have lunch. Lunch should be lighter than breakfast.

Dinner

Your evening meal should be eaten about 4 to 5 hours after lunch, ideally between 5pm and 7pm or no fewer than 3 hours before lying down for bedtime. Late-night eating is connected to a higher likelihood of picking unhealthy food options (see the box on page 4).

PROTEIN AND FIBRE

It's good to incorporate meat, fish, eggs, beans and other non-dairy sources of protein into your diet. Eat at least two portions of fish a week, including a portion of oily fish (but don't eat fish every day).

Eating foods rich in fibre can be helpful for your digestion. Constipation tends to become more of a nuisance as you get older, but fibre-rich foods can help prevent this and other digestive problems.

OILS

Extra virgin olive oil is known for its prominent role in the Mediterranean diet, and it is high in healthy monounsaturated fatty acids and antioxidants. It works well with savoury dishes containing vegetables, poultry and fish. For olive oil to be certified extra virgin, it must be cold pressed. Cold pressed indicates that the olives never exceed a certain temperature during the pressing process when the oil is extracted, which ensures maximum nutritional quality.

Vegetable oils lack the antioxidants that are found in extra virgin olive oil and it is not always obvious what the source vegetable is, so it is best to avoid vegetable oil if possible.

Sunflower oil is very nutrient dense and may be beneficial to our health. Sunflower oil is made from the pressed seeds of sunflowers. It's high in vitamin A, which is a powerful antioxidant that is known to protect the health of our cells, tissues and organs and may play a part in boosting our immune system. Research has shown that including sunflower oil in our diet can effectively lower our total cholesterol levels.

Grapeseed oil is high in heart-healthy polyunsaturated fats including omega 3s and omega 6s.

It's best to consume all oils in moderation, as oils are fats and are therefore high in calories. Use a variety of oils in your diet to maximise the health benefits that each oil offers and use measuring spoons when using oil in cooking.

IRON

Iron is important for our general health. A lack of iron can make us feel as if we have no energy, so regularly include iron-rich foods in your diet such as spinach and broccoli, other green vegetables, nuts, seeds, grains, whole wheat, brown rice, fortified breakfast cereals and some dried fruit. Iron is also found in legumes such as peas, beans and lentils, oily fish such as sardines, and eggs. The best source of iron is lean red meat, as the iron in animal-based foods is easier to absorb than the iron in plant-based foods. If you are a vegetarian or vegan, you need to take extra care with your diet to ensure you get enough iron. Bear in mind that consuming coffee, tea, wine and dairy beverages can reduce iron absorption. If you can, have these between meals, rather than with your meal.

SALT

Too much salt can raise your blood pressure, which puts you at an increased risk of health problems such as heart disease or a stroke.

Most of the salt we eat is already in foods such as cereals, bread, tinned soups and other ready-prepared foods. Check food labels before you buy and choose ones that contain less salt. Try to avoid adding salt when cooking your food.

VITAMIN D

Vitamin D is important for bone, teeth and muscle health and to help prevent osteoporosis. The body creates vitamin D from exposure to direct sunlight on the skin when outdoors. It is also found in oily fish, red meat, liver, eggs, and some breakfast cereals and dietary supplements. Make sure you check whether the latter is suitable for you by consulting your doctor, as consuming too much vitamin D from supplements over a long period of time could cause excess build-up of calcium.

WEIGHT

If you're overweight, you'll become less mobile as you grow older. This can affect your health and quality of life. Being overweight also increases your risk of diseases such as heart disease and diabetes.

Being underweight isn't healthy either and may be a sign that you're not eating enough or that you're unwell. Being underweight also increases your risk of osteoporosis.

If you're worried about your weight, ask your doctor to check it. They may refer you to a dietitian, who can advise you about changing what you eat to meet your current needs.

Do watch out for lack of appetite. It is important to get all the energy and nutrients that your body needs. If you don't eat as much as you used to, eat smaller meals more often and supplement them with nutritious snacks, such as vegetables, fruits and wholegrain toast.

You may eat less because you find it more difficult to buy or prepare food, or because you find it harder to get around if you have a condition such as arthritis.

Eat regularly, at least three times a day. If you don't feel like cooking from scratch, have a tinned, chilled or frozen ready-prepared meal instead. It's a good idea to have a store of foods in the freezer and cupboard just in case you cannot go out.

PORTION CONTROL

Instead of counting calories and relying on numbers, try this hand-measuring guide for main meals.

A serving of protein (20–30g) = 1 palmful
A serving of vegetables = 1 fistful
A serving of carbohydrates (20–30g) = 1 cupped handful
A serving of fats (7–12g) = 1 thumb

DRINK MORE WATER

Drink plenty of fluids every day to keep yourself hydrated. Aim to drink at least six times a day, and more in warmer weather or if you're exercising. Tea, mineral water, soda water and reduced-fat milk can all count towards your fluid intake during the day, but regular water is always best.

Drinks that contain a lot of caffeine, such as strong tea or coffee, might make your body produce more urine. If you mostly drink strong tea and coffee, make sure you also drink some water or other fluids each day that don't contain caffeine. Soups can boost your fluid intake (see page 73).

Try to avoid adding sugar to tea or coffee. You could start by reducing the amount of sugar by half and then gradually removing sugar altogether to allow your taste buds time to adjust.

Avoid drinking too many soft drinks, especially fizzy ones.

THE 'BIG FOUR', GLUCOSE AND DIABETES

The body needs four essential nutrients to keep healthy: fats, protein, vitamins and minerals. Water and fibre are not nutrients but they are essential to life. Too much or too little of any of the nutrients may not be good for the body.

A fifth nutrient is carbohydrate but it is not essential to life, as the body can use protein and fat to make all the glucose it requires for energy. All food and drink that contain carbohydrate, including brown and white bread, rice, pasta, potatoes, sugar, cakes, confectionary and sugar-sweetened beverages break down and release glucose into the blood. Carbohydrate is the only nutrient that directly increases blood glucose levels and is therefore important in blood glucose control.

Did you know that we should only have 5g (1 teaspoon) of glucose in our blood at any time? Diabetes is a condition in which the amount of glucose in the blood at diagnosis is too high because the body cannot use the glucose as energy.

Insulin is a hormone made by the body that allows the body to convert glucose into energy. Type 1 diabetes occurs when the body does not produce enough insulin. Pre-diabetes and Type 2 diabetes occur when the body is still able to make insulin but it cannot use it properly. This is called insulin resistance. No matter the type of diabetes, the end result is that glucose stays in the blood and cannot be converted into energy, causing tiredness, hunger, thirstiness and a multitude of health problems.

There is strong evidence that individuals with pre-diabetes or Type 2 diabetes can make changes to their lifestyle – such as reducing intake of refined and processed carbohydrates – that can enable their blood glucose to return to what would be considered normal while also omitting all diabetes medication. This would be classed as remission.

Although people with Type 1 diabetes cannot go into remission, they can improve their blood glucose control and reduce episodes of low and high blood glucose levels. However, it is important to recognise that things can deteriorate again if they revert to their previous lifestyle.

Helpful hints

PLANNING AHEAD

- Whenever possible, plan your meals ahead. This enables you to do some preparation in advance, eat nutritious food and have your meals at optimal times. Before shopping, make a shopping list – this will help prevent you from spending money on unnecessary processed, sugary and salty products.

AT THE SHOPS

- The measures in all the recipes in this book are approximate, so don't worry if the size of tin or jar you buy differs slightly from the one that is used in the book. The only time you need to be more careful with quantities is when you are cooking rice or baking.
- Make a habit of reading labels and ingredients lists when you're shopping. Perhaps take a small magnifying glass with you to the shops. Remember that ingredients are listed by quantity from the highest to the lowest amount. This means that the first ingredient is what the manufacturer used the most of. A good guide is to scan the first three ingredients as they make up the largest part of what you're eating. In addition, any ingredients list that is more than two to three lines long suggests that the product is highly processed.
- Buy your local supermarket's economy version of products such as baked beans, kidney beans, spaghetti, pasta and rice whenever possible, to make savings. Beware of buying a smaller tin of food that is actually more expensive than the bigger size.
- Remember that frozen vegetables are as nutritious as fresh.
- Bear in mind that if you purchase chocolates, desserts or sweets, anything labelled as 'low fat' could contain a large amount of sugar.

IN THE KITCHEN

- Make sure that if a recipe says 'simmer gently', that this is what you do, otherwise you could end up with a burnt pan and food.
- Some bread, rice, potatoes and other starchy foods are good – use wholegrain varieties when possible.
- If you have half a tin of something leftover, transfer it to a covered container – a pudding bowl with a plate over it will do – and keep it in the fridge. If left in the tin, it may develop a metallic taste.

IT'S ALL ABOUT BALANCE

Your body changes as you get older, but a balanced diet will help you stay healthy. A diet high in fresh fruit and vegetables, whole grains, pulses, fish, nuts, seeds and oils such as olive oil, but low in saturated and trans fats and processed foods, is likely to provide the best combination of nutrients in the optimal amounts to help protect your body and your brain. It is important to include a good range of foods in your diet. Try not to eat too much of any one food.

Food is fuel and hot meals and drinks help keep you warm.

Keep active by taking some exercise, but do not at any time exert yourself physically to an extent far beyond what you are accustomed to. Drink alcohol only in moderation, do not smoke cigarettes and try to avoid stress as much as you can. It's okay to seek support if you're not content or are finding it difficult to cope with the situation you're in. Loneliness and isolation can have a serious affect on your health and can lead to depression and a decline in overall wellbeing, so it is important to connect with friends, family and the wider community: smile at others when you get a chance, even the cashier at the shop or the person sitting next to you in the doctor's waiting room; call a friend or relative (it could be the next best thing to being with them); and get involved in local community activities – the chances are you'll have access to groups that would be of personal interest to you. Even start a diary – this can help you feel less lonely, as you could plan the week ahead and put things in your diary to look forward to each day, such as a walk or going to the library or coffee shop. A diary is also helpful for writing down the meals you are planning to make and keeping tabs on what, when and how you eat.

Eating healthily to fuel the mind and the body improves our mood, reduces stress and can lead to thinking positively. And people who engage in positive thinking experience increased lifespan, lower rates of depression, resistance to colds, better cardiovascular health and better coping skills during tough times. Trying something new, such as cooking a recipe you've not tried before, can break monotony not only in your eating habits, but also your lifestyle, with an added feel-good factor.

CHEW YOUR FOOD

Studies have shown that eating meals slowly leads to reduced energy intake, which is a good thing if you're trying to lose weight or maintain a healthy weight.

From the time you begin eating, it takes about 20 minutes for the stomach to signal to the brain that it is satisfied. When we eat too fast, we don't give our brains enough time to realise that we are full, and usually end up eating way more than we need. Slow eating is all about chewing food thoroughly. Soft foods should be chewed about 7 to 8 times and denser foods like raw vegetables and meat around 30 times. Chewing properly breaks down large pieces of food into smaller chunks, thus enabling the enzymes in saliva to do their job and putting less stress and strain on the stomach. Eating too fast and overeating could contribute to digestive problems and chewing food properly also reduces the risk of choking.

Fall in love with food

Cooking is one of the most common hobbies that people take up during retirement. During some of the busier periods of your life, you may have found that cooking was pushed aside and, rather than create meals that included some of your favourite ingredients, you opted for quick meals to satiate your family. Now that you have some extra time on your hands, spending that time cooking is a great way to maintain your mental and physical health. Replacing the simple family recipes that got you through busy times with something slightly more indulgent allows you to reignite the spark that food once gave you while allowing you to channel your energy into something productive.

As you get older, food may not taste as strong as it once did. Therefore, you might need to try new types of food and ways of cooking in order to feel as satisfied as you once would have been. However, this can be difficult, especially if you haven't prepared food from scratch in a while. This is why it is important to invest in a few cookbooks that can help you to prepare dishes with strong flavour profiles that you love.

Food should be something to be enjoyed at any age, which is why I have created some recipes to help you cook healthy and nutritious meals. Whether you're looking for some cooking inspiration for yourself or a loved one, these recipes should give you plenty of ideas for delicious food you can make easily at home.

The Seasoned Foodie is a collection of simple dishes that are easy to follow, however young you feel. In addition to general dietary hints and tips, you will find more than 100 mouthwatering recipes. These recipes have been gathered over the past few years during my time teaching healthy cooking at Open Age, a charity in London that champions an active life for older people. They provide a wide range of physical, creative and mentally stimulating programmes to enable older people to develop new skills, fulfil their potential and make new friends. The cooking sessions involve preparing, cooking and serving the dishes within 90 minutes. The recipes in this book have been tried and tested by the seasoned cooks at Open Age and can be made with ease within this timeframe and with a little planning.

The recipes are highly flavoursome, taste great and are nutritious too. They are low in salt and sugar and maximise flavour, using fresh herbs, spices and plenty of fruit and vegetables.

The book is divided into seven chapters: Breakfast, Lunch, Soups, Salads, Sides, Dips and Dunks, Dinner, and Desserts.

Whether you want a warming curry to see you through a chilly winter evening or a sumptuous supper packed with fresh herbs, this is a comprehensive selection of recipes for every occasion. In addition to the recipes, you will find kitchen and cooking hacks, shopping suggestions and information about the importance of having a balanced diet and eating better to stay healthier for longer.

Store-cupboard essentials

Tinned food and other store-cupboard ingredients
Baked beans
Baking powder
Balsamic vinegar
Brown and white basmati rice
Black peppercorns
Caster sugar
Chickpeas
Chopped tomatoes
Chilli flakes and chilli powder
Chinese five-spice powder
Cornflour
Curry powder (any brand)
Dijon or English mustard
Dried mixed fruits
Dried mixed herbs
Dried oregano
Dried thyme
Free-range eggs
Fruit cocktail
Ground cinnamon
Ground cumin
Ground turmeric
Low-fat mayonnaise
Low-sodium or low-salt stock cubes
Mackerel fillets
Olive oil, rapeseed, sesame, groundnut, grapeseed
    or sunflower oil

Peanut butter
Ready-made custard
Red and brown lentils
Smoked paprika
Soy sauce (preferably low-sodium or low-salt)
Tinned beans (any variety)
Tomato purée or paste
Tuna
White flour pasta
Wholewheat or wholegrain pasta
Wholemeal pitta breads
Wholemeal plain flour
Worcestershire sauce

Fruit, vegetables, poultry, fish and herbs

Apples
Avocados
Berries (frozen or fresh) such as blueberries,
    blackberries, strawberries
Carrots
Cabbage
Celery
Fresh broccoli
Frozen fish such as salmon or cod, or a fish medley
Frozen mixed vegetables such as broccoli, carrots and spinach
Frozen petits pois or garden peas
Frozen skinless and boneless chicken portions
Garlic
Green beans (fresh or frozen)
Leeks
Lemons
Lettuce or salad leaves
Limes
Onions
Pears

Plums
Pomegranates
Potatoes and sweet potatoes
Red onions
Tangerines or easy peelers
Thyme and other fresh herbs
Tomatoes

Dairy

Greek-style yogurt
Hard cheese such as Cheddar (small matchbox-sized portion
  per serving)
Light salad cheese
Reduced-fat cottage cheese
Reduced-fat soured cream
Reduced-fat crème fraîche
Semi-skimmed milk
Single cream

Kit

Essential kit
Baking tray
Chopping boards x 2 (one for vegetables and one for meat
  and poultry)
Cutlery
Crockery
Frying pan (ideally non-stick)
Gloves for washing up
Knife
Knife sharpener
Large saucepan with lid
Peeler
Pepper mill
Slotted spoon or a fish slice

Small casserole dish
Small saucepan
Spoon for stirring
Tea towel
Tin opener

Really useful items
Cheese grater
Colander or sieve
Garlic press or crusher
Measuring spoons and jugs
Mixing bowl
Rubber spatula
Small square cake tin
Weighing scales or machine
Whisk

Handy items
An electric stick blender
A small food processor
An electric hand mixer for mixing batter for cakes
1-cup kettle
Spice mill or a pestle and mortar

Luxury item
Handheld milk frother

Breakfast

You have probably heard many times that breakfast is the most important meal of the day. That's because you determine the pattern for your blood sugar for the rest of the day with your first meal. It's advised to eat within the first hour of waking up to get your body prepared for the rest of the day. So, between 6am and 10am is a good window to eat your breakfast.

Evidence suggests that our bodies may function better when we eat more in the morning than at night, a pattern that's vastly different from how many of us actually eat. Timing our meals this way may lead to healthier body weight, better hormone regulation, reduced blood sugar and cholesterol levels and good sleep.

Try to avoid foods such as pastries or beverages with sugar, which could result in blood sugar spikes and set you up for a series of highs and lows for the rest of the day. A combination of whole grains, protein and fat such as wholewheat toast with a small dollop of peanut butter and some fresh berries would be preferable.

Wholewheat bread contains the bran, the germ and the endosperm of the wheat kernels and is a healthier choice than refined white wheat bread. Similar to wholewheat bread, wholegrain bread can be made up of grains such as whole barley, wholegrain oats and rolled oats, amongst others. When purchasing bread, try to opt for wholegrain or wholewheat bread which are the least processed or refined.

Turmeric Latte

Turmeric is a spice that's known to calm inflammation because it contains curcumin. This strong antioxidant is better absorbed into the bloodstream when it is consumed with black pepper. Cinnamon also possesses anti-inflammatory properties, and may improve some key risk factors for heart disease, raised cholesterol and high blood pressure.

SERVES 2
350ml semi-skimmed or plant milk
¼ tsp ground turmeric
Pinch of ground cinnamon
Pinch of ground ginger
Pinch of freshly ground black pepper
½ tsp vanilla extract (optional)
1 tsp runny honey

1   Put all the ingredients in a saucepan and whisk constantly over a gentle heat, ideally with a handheld milk frother if you have one. Once hot, pour into two mugs.

Cooked Apple Stew for Muesli

Apples are extremely rich in antioxidants, flavonoids and dietary fibre (if the skin is left on). Including the cinnamon on colder days adds a warm, sweet touch of spice to the apples.

Serve warm with 2 tablespoons of single cream and 6 tablespoons of muesli.

SERVES 2

1 tsp unsalted butter
2 cooking apples, washed, cores removed and chopped
2 prunes, chopped
1 tsp brown sugar
Pinch of ground cinnamon

1   Melt the butter in a saucepan over a medium heat. Add the apples and cook for 5–10 minutes until softened. Add the prunes and cook for 1 more minute. Add the sugar and the cinnamon and cook for another 2 minutes.
2   Remove from the heat and serve.
3   The apple stew can be stored in an airtight container in the fridge for up to 4 days, or frozen in an airtight container for up to 6–8 months.

Spinach and Mushroom Omelette

The vibrant colours of the spinach combined with the shallots flavoured with thyme make this an out-of-the-ordinary omelette. Spinach is rich in vitamin K, folate and fibre, which may benefit digestion. However, if you're prone to kidney stones, you may want to replace the spinach with a few chopped chives and some grated cheese.

SERVES 2

1 tbsp extra virgin olive oil
2 shallots, chopped
115g mushrooms, wiped clean and thinly sliced
Sprig of thyme, washed
100g baby spinach leaves, washed
¼ tsp freshly ground black pepper
4 free-range eggs
1 tbsp unsalted butter

1   Heat the oil in a non-stick frying pan over a medium-high heat and swirl to coat, then tip in the shallots, mushrooms and thyme sprig. Sauté for 7 minutes, or until the mushrooms are browned, then tip in the spinach and sauté for 4 minutes until the liquid almost evaporates. Remove the mixture from the pan and discard the thyme sprig. Remove the pan from the heat and wipe the pan clean with kitchen paper.

2   Whisk the pepper and the eggs in a small bowl.

3   Return the wiped-out pan to a medium heat. Add the butter and swirl to coat. Add half of the egg mixture and cook for 1 minute, then lift the edges of the omelette with a rubber spatula, tilting the pan to allow the uncooked egg onto the bottom of the pan. Cook for another minute or until the centre just begins to set but is still very soft.

4 Arrange half of the mushroom and spinach mixture over the middle of the omelette. Run the spatula around the edges and under the omelette to loosen it from the pan, then fold it in half. Carefully slide the omelette onto a plate.

5 Repeat with the remaining ingredients and serve.

Baked Beans Egg Bake

This recipe is similar to a dish from the Middle East known as shakshuka, flavoured with cumin and chilli (amongst other spices). The recipe below is a lighter version.

SERVES 2

1 tbsp rapeseed or extra virgin olive oil
1 red pepper, deseeded and thinly sliced
½ red onion, sliced
½ tsp sweet smoked paprika
200g tinned chopped tomatoes
415g tin baked beans
2 free-range eggs
Pinch of freshly ground black pepper

To serve
2 slices of sourdough bread
50g light salad cheese
A few chives, washed and snipped (optional)

1   Heat the oil in a frying pan (that has a lid) over a medium heat, tip in the pepper and onion and cook for 2 minutes until softened. Sprinkle in the paprika and cook for another minute, then mix in the tomatoes and cook for 2–3 minutes until the mixture has thickened. Add the beans and cook for a further 4–5 minutes, then make two wells in the mixture and break the eggs into the wells. Cover with a lid and cook for 6–8 minutes until the whites have set and the yolks are still runny (or cooked to your liking).

2   Sprinkle the black pepper over the eggs. Toast the bread and crumble the salad cheese over it. Scatter the snipped chives, if using, on top of the cheese and serve with the egg bake.

Avocado on Toast

Although it's predominantly used in savoury dishes, the avocado is a fruit. Native to Central and South America, it's loaded with healthy monounsaturated fatty acids known to help reduce inflammation and cholesterol levels. This dish makes a refreshing change to eggs on toast.

SERVES 1

1 ripe avocado
Juice of ½ lemon
Generous pinch of freshly ground black pepper
Pinch of chilli flakes (optional)
1 slice of bread, preferably wholemeal
1 tsp extra virgin olive oil

1   Just before eating, cut the avocado in half and remove the stone. Scoop out the flesh into a bowl and add the lemon juice. Using a fork, mash the mixture and tip in the black pepper and the chilli flakes, if using.
2   Toast the bread, then drizzle it with the oil. Put the avocado mash on top of the toast and serve immediately.

Cheese and Tomato Toastie

Packed with lycopene, which is a powerful antioxidant that can lower the risk of certain types of cancer, tomatoes are also a great source of immunity-boosting vitamin C.

Serve this toastie with chilli sauce or ketchup, or a crisp green salad – it works just as well for lunch as it does for breakfast.

SERVES 1

1 tbsp mayonnaise
2 slices of wholemeal bread
2 tsp unsalted butter
1 tomato, washed and finely chopped
2 tbsp grated Cheddar cheese
Generous pinch of freshly ground black pepper

1   Spread the mayonnaise on one side of each slice of bread.
2   Melt 1 teaspoon of the butter in a frying pan over a medium heat, then add one slice of the bread, mayonnaise side facing up. Cook for about 2 minutes, then add the chopped tomato, evenly spreading the pieces over the bread slice. Sprinkle the cheese on top, followed by the black pepper. Put the other slice of bread on top with the mayonnaise side touching the tomato and cheese filling. Press down with a flat spatula, then carefully flip the complete sandwich over to cook the other side. You could use a fish slice along with the spatula to make it easier to turn the sandwich over.
3   Add the remaining teaspoon of butter and cook for 2 minutes more until the cheese has melted and the bread has browned. Carefully remove from the pan and serve.

Oat and Ginger Cookies

Oats are incredibly nutritious and are higher in protein than most grains. They can help lower cholesterol levels and improve blood sugar control. These cookies are a wonderful occasional treat – they are very filling and work well as a breakfast cookie with a nice cuppa in the morning.

MAKES 10-15 COOKIES
65g unsalted butter
70g brown or light muscovado sugar
Pinch of bicarbonate of soda
½ tsp ground ginger
2 tbsp finely chopped stem ginger
2 tsp peeled and grated root ginger
75g plain flour
75g rolled oats

1 Preheat the oven to 180°C/350°F/Gas 4 and line a baking tray or sheet with greaseproof paper.
2 Melt the butter and mix with the sugar in a bowl. Add the bicarbonate of soda and all the ginger and combine well. Stir in the plain flour and the rolled oats to make a firm dough, then roll into 10–15 small golf-ball sized pieces. Space out the pieces of dough on the lined tray or sheet and bake in the oven for 10–12 minutes until lightly golden.
3 Remove from the oven and allow the cookies to firm up a little, then transfer to a wire rack to cool completely. Store in an airtight container. They will keep for up to 10 days.

Eggless Oat Muffins

These muffins make a welcome change to a daily egg-based breakfast. Oats are gluten-free grains and they help reduce cholesterol and the risk of heart disease, lower blood sugar levels, and increase the feeling of fullness.

You can make your own oat flour by blitzing whole oats in a blender for about a minute until finely ground.

MAKES 8-10 MUFFINS

200g oat flour
1 tsp baking powder
½ tsp bicarbonate of soda
½ tsp ground cinnamon
¼ cup crushed walnuts (optional)
1 large ripe banana
225ml apple sauce
120ml almond or semi-skimmed milk
1 tbsp vanilla extract
1 tsp apple cider vinegar
80g caster sugar, maple syrup, or finely chopped
   or mashed dates

1   Preheat the oven to 180°C/350°F/Gas 4.
2   In a large bowl, mix together the oat flour, baking powder, bicarbonate of soda and cinnamon, adding the caster sugar if using it instead of wet sweetener and the walnuts, if using.
3   Peel the banana then mash it with a fork or potato masher in a medium bowl. Add the apple sauce, milk, vanilla, vinegar, and maple syrup or date paste (if using a wet sweetener) and whisk together.

4   Pour the well-blended wet mixture into the large bowl with the dry ingredients and fold together gently until well combined. It's okay if it looks a bit runny. Spoon or scoop the batter into 8–10 holes of a silicone muffin non-stick baking pan or 8–10 silicone muffin cases in a muffin tin.

5   Bake in the oven for 25 minutes, until firm on top.

6   Remove from the oven and allow to cool. The muffins can be frozen in sealed bags for up to 3 months (defrost thoroughly before eating).

Spiced Hot Chocolate

Dark chocolate that has a high cocoa content is loaded with antioxidants. Do be mindful, however, that even this variety of chocolate does contain sugar so is best consumed in moderation. If you want to reduce your caffeine intake in the morning, this can be a once-in-a-while replacement for your coffee.

SERVES 2

40g dark chocolate (85% cocoa solids), broken into
  small pieces
40g unsweetened cocoa powder
250ml semi-skimmed milk or plant milk
1/8 tsp ground cinnamon
A few dark chocolate gratings, to serve

1 Place the broken chocolate in a small heavy-based saucepan over a low heat with all the other ingredients. Simmer gently for 5 minutes, whisking occasionally, until the chocolate has melted. Strain the mixture through a nylon sieve and serve immediately in small espresso cups, sprinkled with a few chocolate gratings.

Tomato Bruschetta

Tomatoes are packed with lycopene that helps reduce the risk of heart disease and cancer. They also possess anti-viral properties that are key for all functions of the immune system. If you can get hold of a wholemeal baguette for this recipe, that's even better, for increased fibre intake.

Make the tomato mixture an hour or so before serving – it will give the flavours time to mingle and develop. This recipe works just as well for lunch as it does for breakfast.

SERVES 2

½ small red onion, finely chopped
2 medium tomatoes, roughly chopped and drained
1 garlic clove, crushed, or 1 tsp garlic purée
4–6 fresh basil leaves, washed and finely chopped
2 tbsp balsamic vinegar
2 tbsp extra virgin olive oil
Generous pinch of freshly ground black pepper
1 small crusty baguette

1 In a large bowl, mix the onion, tomatoes, garlic and basil using a large spoon, taking care not to mash or break up the tomatoes too much. Add the balsamic vinegar, olive oil and black pepper and mix again. If you have time, cover and chill the mixture in the fridge for at least 1 hour. This will allow the flavours to settle and blend together.

2 Slice the baguette diagonally into thick slices and lightly toast the slices until they are light brown on both sides.

3 Serve the mixture on the warm slices of bread. If you prefer the mixture at room temperature, remove it from the fridge 30 minutes before serving.

Cheesy Buckwheat Blinis

Despite its name, buckwheat is not related to wheat and is gluten-free. It has a high mineral and antioxidant content and may help improve blood sugar levels and colon health. This recipe makes breakfast time that little bit extra special with a serving of smoked salmon.

SERVES 2

40g buckwheat flour
Generous pinch of baking powder
¼ tsp freshly ground black pepper
A generous pinch of turmeric
75ml semi-skimmed or plant-based milk
½ tsp Dijon mustard
30g Cheddar cheese, grated
Small handful of chives, washed and snipped
1 free-range egg white (keep the yolk for the scrambled eggs)
Pinch of salt
Knob of unsalted butter

For the scrambled eggs
2 free-range eggs (plus the extra egg yolk)
Generous pinch of freshly ground black pepper
Knob of unsalted butter

To serve
125g smoked salmon
½ lemon, cut into wedges

1   To make the blini batter, stir together the buckwheat flour, baking powder, black pepper, turmeric and the milk to make a smooth batter. Add the mustard, grated cheese and chives and mix until well combined.

2   In a separate bowl, whisk the egg white with a pinch of salt until soft peaks form when the whisk is removed. Adding a little salt to the egg white helps achieve higher peaks.

3   A little at a time, fold the whisked egg white into the blini batter mixture using a metal spoon.

4   Melt the butter in a frying pan over a medium-high heat then scoop large tablespoons of the batter into the pan to make medium-sized blinis (about 10cm in diameter) – you will need to cook them in batches, and the mixture should make 4 blinis in total. Fry for 2–3 minutes until small bubbles appear on the surface and the underside is not runny. Turn the blini over and cook on the other side for a further 1–2 minutes, or until golden brown. Keep the cooked blinis warm by placing them in the oven on a low heat and repeat until all of the mixture is used up.

5   To make the scrambled eggs, whisk the eggs and extra egg yolk in a bowl and add the black pepper. Melt the butter in a small saucepan over a medium heat, then pour in the eggs, stirring a little to break the eggs up slightly as they set. Cook for 1–2 minutes, then remove the pan from the heat and set the eggs aside to finish cooking in the residual heat for a further 1–2 minutes.

6   To serve, place 2 blinis onto each serving plate. Top with the scrambled eggs. Arrange the smoked salmon on the side of the blinis and serve with the lemon wedges.

Lunch

As our metabolism peaks each day between the hours of 10am and 2pm, and our digestive function is at its strongest, it's recommended to have lunch during that timeframe. Skipping lunch can lead us to eat more later in the evening, which can interfere with restful sleep and also cause a drop in blood sugars, resulting in dizziness. If you're not feeling hungry, it is better to eat a little than to skip lunch entirely.

Baked Beans with Cumin and Paprika

Baked beans are made with white beans such as haricot or cannellini beans. They're cooked in a tomato sauce which, more often than not, contains salt and sugar, so do read the label to check the amounts. Roughly three heaped tablespoons of baked beans (about 200g, or half a tin of shop-bought) can count as one of your five a day.

Serve hot on a jacket potato.

SERVES 2

1 tbsp extra virgin olive oil
1 onion, finely chopped
½ tsp ground cumin
½ tsp sweet or hot paprika
200g tinned chopped tomatoes
415g tin baked beans
1 tsp Worcestershire sauce (optional)

1   Heat the oil in a saucepan over a medium heat, add the onion and cook gently for 5–7 minutes until softened. Tip in the cumin and paprika and mix well, then add the tomatoes and cook gently for a further 5 minutes until the tomatoes are softened and pulpy. Stir in the baked beans and cook for a couple of minutes, then stir in 60ml water and mix well. Add the Worcestershire sauce, if using, and cook for a further 5 minutes. Remove from the heat and serve hot.

Brazilian-style Black Beans

Black turtle beans, or simply 'black beans' for short, are especially common in Latin American cuisine. High in fibre and packed with nutrients, they're a healthy addition to any dish. If you can't find tinned black beans, use dried, making sure that you soak them overnight then cook them thoroughly before following the recipe below.

Serve with Tunisian-style Aubergines and rice.

SERVES 6

1 tbsp extra virgin olive oil
1 onion, chopped
2 garlic cloves, chopped
1 green chilli, chopped
400g tin black beans, drained and rinsed
500ml vegetable stock (can be made from a low-sodium or low-salt stock cube, or see recipe on page 74)

To serve
¼ tsp freshly ground black pepper
A few coriander leaves

1 Heat the oil in a large frying pan over a medium heat, add the onion and sauté for 5–7 minutes until softened and lightly golden. Add the garlic and stir, then tip in the green chilli and cook for a couple of minutes. Stir in the beans and cook for 3 minutes, then add the stock and simmer uncovered for 7–8 minutes until the sauce is thick. Sprinkle over the black pepper and the coriander leaves and serve.

Tofu Stir-Fry

Any kind of stir-fry is quick and easy to make and is a great way of incorporating lots of fresh vegetables into a dish.

Tofu is made from compressing soya milk to create solid blocks. It is high in protein and contains several anti-inflammatory antioxidant phytochemicals, in addition to fibre, potassium, magnesium, iron, copper and manganese.

SERVES 2

For the sauce

1 tsp toasted sesame oil

2 tbsp low-sodium (low-salt) soy sauce

1 tsp runny honey

1 tsp sriracha sauce

1 tsp oyster sauce

1 garlic clove, crushed or finely chopped, or 1 tsp garlic purée

Generous pinch of freshly ground black pepper

For the stir-fry

250g udon noodles

1 tsp toasted sesame oil

1 tsp extra virgin olive oil or sunflower oil

180g firm tofu, cut into 2.5cm pieces

2 spring onions, washed and finely chopped

80g broccoli florets

1 red pepper, deseeded and thinly sliced

4–6 mushrooms, wiped clean and thinly sliced

1. Place the sauce ingredients in a bowl and whisk together with 2 tablespoons of water. Set aside.
2. Cook the noodles according to the instructions on the packet, then drain and rinse under a cold tap.
3. Heat a large frying pan or wok over a medium heat and add the sesame oil and olive oil or sunflower oil. Add the tofu and cook for about 5 minutes until lightly browned all over, then remove from the pan and set aside. Add the spring onions to the pan and cook for a minute to soften them a little, then tip in the broccoli florets and stir-fry for 2 minutes. Add the red pepper and mushrooms and continue sautéing until the pepper starts to soften and the mushrooms begin to brown. Add the cooked noodles to the pan, pour in the sauce, toss and cook for 2–3 minutes, then remove from the heat. Serve immediately. You can store any leftovers in an airtight container in the fridge for up to 3 days.

Scandi-style Salmon with Potato and Pickle Salad

Dill is a gently sweet herb that goes well with most fish dishes and appears frequently in Scandinavian recipes.

Your body requires protein to heal, protect bone health and prevent muscle loss. Salmon is a high-quality protein source and is also rich in omega 3 fatty acids which have been shown to reduce inflammation, lower blood pressure and decrease risk factors for disease.

SERVES 2

For the salmon

2 salmon fillets

Grated zest of ½ unwaxed lemon

4 tbsp demerara sugar

1 tbsp washed and roughly chopped dill

For the salad

300g new potatoes

3–4 gherkins, drained and finely diced

2 tbsp mayonnaise

¼ tsp ground white pepper

1 tbsp washed and roughly chopped dill, plus extra fronds to serve (if liked)

1 Put the salmon skin side down in a small baking dish. Combine the lemon zest, sugar and tablespoon of chopped dill and pat the mixture all over the salmon flesh. Cover and set aside for 30 minutes.
2 Meanwhile, cook the potatoes for the salad in boiling water until tender, then drain. Return to the pan and gently crush against the side of the pan with the back of a fork. Leave to cool to room temperature, then mix with the rest of the ingredients for the salad.
3 Preheat the oven to 220°C/420°F/Gas 7.
4 Bake the salmon in the oven for 10–15 minutes until just cooked.
5 Serve the salmon with the potato salad and a little extra dill if you like.

Spiced Aubergines with Black-eyed Beans

Black-eyed beans contain energy-boosting B vitamins and selenium, which is needed to produce antibodies to help prevent cancer. A pinch of the spice asafoetida (see page 52) added to bean and lentil dishes can help reduce any bloated feelings.

Serve this dish hot, with wholemeal pitta bread.

SERVES 2

400g tin black-eyed beans, drained, or 100g dried
   black-eyed beans

1 tbsp sunflower oil

½ tsp brown or black mustard seeds

Generous pinch of asafoetida

1 aubergine (about 300g), washed and cut into 2.5cm cubes

½ tsp ground turmeric

1 tsp ground cumin

1 tsp ground coriander

Pinch of chilli powder

Pinch of sea salt

1 tsp peeled and grated root ginger or ginger paste

A few washed and chopped coriander leaves, to serve

1 If using dried beans, cook them according to the instructions on the packet.
2 Heat the sunflower oil in a large saucepan over a medium heat and add the mustard seeds followed by the asafoetida. Once the seeds crackle, tip in the cubed aubergine and sauté for 2 minutes until nicely glazed. Stir in the turmeric, cumin, ground coriander, chilli powder and salt. Reduce the heat to low, cover and simmer for 5–7 minutes to steam the aubergine. Add the cooked black-eyed beans and cook, covered, for a further 3–4 minutes until well combined. Stir in the ginger and mix well.
3 Remove from the heat, sprinkle over the coriander leaves and serve hot.

Fish Pie

This comforting dish is great for when you have a full house. Feel free to add your favourite herbs, such as dill or parsley.

Sweet potatoes are highly nutritious and a great source of fibre, vitamins C and E, iron and potassium. The orange variety contain more beta-carotene than the yellow and white varieties, which possesses anti-cancer, anti-viral and antioxidant properties.

SERVES 4-6

300g floury potatoes, such as Maris Piper, peeled and halved
400g sweet potatoes, peeled and cut into even pieces
400ml semi-skimmed milk, plus a splash extra
25g unsalted butter, plus a knob
½ tsp freshly ground black pepper
25g plain flour
4–6 spring onions, washed and thinly sliced
320–400g pack of white fish fillets, cut into small pieces
1 tsp Dijon or English mustard
1–2 tbsp washed and finely snipped chives
100g sweetcorn, defrosted if frozen
100g petits pois, defrosted if frozen
100g Cheddar cheese, grated

1   Preheat the oven to 180°C/350°F/Gas 4.
2   Put the potatoes in a saucepan and add enough cold water to cover them. Bring to the boil, then reduce the heat and simmer until tender. Put the sweet potatoes in a separate saucepan and add just enough cold water to cover them. Bring to the boil, then reduce the heat and simmer for 15 minutes, or until tender when pierced with a fork.

3 Drain the potatoes and sweet potatoes and return to one pan on the hob with the burner turned off for a few minutes so the residual heat from the pan will help any excess water evaporate.

4 Put the potatoes and the sweet potatoes into a bowl and mash with a splash of milk and the knob of butter. Mash until quite smooth and well combined, then mix in the black pepper.

5 Melt the 25g of butter in a heavy-based saucepan over a medium heat, add the plain flour and the spring onions, stirring frequently, and cook for 1–2 minutes, then gradually whisk in the 400ml milk, using a fork or balloon whisk if you have one. Bring to the boil and cook for 3–4 minutes, stirring constantly to avoid any lumps and to prevent the mixture sticking to the bottom of the pan, until the mixture has thickened. Remove from the heat and stir in the fish pieces, Dijon or English mustard, chives, sweetcorn and petits pois. Spoon the mixture into an ovenproof dish.

6 Add the potato mash and smooth it over the top of the fish mixture, then sprinkle with the grated cheese. Bake in the oven for 20–25 minutes, or until golden brown on top. You could place the assembled pie in the freezer, covered, then defrost thoroughly and cook it at a later date if you prefer (this dish isn't freezable if you're using pre-frozen fish).

White Cabbage and Potatoes with Red Chilli and Mustard Seeds

Cabbage can be quite bland if it's just boiled. This recipe, however, uses chilli and mustard seeds to give the dish a fiery and spicy boost.

The health benefits of eating cabbage include boosting vitamin C, reducing cholesterol levels and aiding digestion. When choosing white cabbage, pick one that feels heavy for its size and has unblemished, smooth leaves.

Serve with wholemeal pitta breads and a mixed green salad.

SERVES 2

200g white cabbage, shredded and washed
1 tbsp extra virgin olive oil or sunflower oil
¼ tsp brown or black mustard seeds
1 dried red chilli or ¼ tsp chilli flakes
100g potatoes (about 1 medium potato), peeled and
    cut into small pieces
¼ tsp sea salt

1   Steam the cabbage for 5 minutes until a little soft, then set aside. To steam the cabbage in the microwave, place it in a small microwave-safe casserole dish, add about 5mm depth of water, cover and microwave on high for about 8 minutes. If your microwave doesn't have a turntable, rotate the dish a quarter-turn halfway through cooking. Drain the water from the dish.

2   Heat the oil in a saucepan over a medium heat and add a few of the mustard seeds, and when they crackle add the remaining seeds. Tip in the chilli or chilli flakes and mix. Add the potato and sauté for 5–7 minutes until the potato pieces are soft. Mix in the salt then tip in the steamed cabbage. Stir-fry for 3–4 minutes. Serve with wholemeal pitta breads and a mixed green salad, removing the whole dried chilli if using.

Fusilli with Mushrooms

Fusilli is a short twisted or spiral-shaped pasta that is usually served with a tomato-based sauce, but I've created a creamier mushroom-based sauce that works just as well in terms of flavour.

The niacin in mushrooms is good for the digestive system and recent studies have shown that eating one portion of mushrooms a week may reduce the likelihood of mild cognitive decline.

SERVES 2

100g fusilli pasta
3 tbsp olive oil
1 onion, finely chopped
2 garlic cloves, finely chopped
250g button mushrooms, wiped clean and thinly sliced
2 tbsp crème fraîche or soured cream
A few sprigs of flat-leaf parsley, washed and roughly chopped
¼ tsp freshly ground black pepper
Pinch of chilli flakes

1   Cook the pasta in plenty of fresh boiling water until it is tender but still al dente (firm to the bite) – this should take about 10 minutes. Drain in a colander and run the pasta under a cold tap. This prevents the pasta from sticking together.
2   Heat the olive oil in a frying pan over a medium heat, add the onion and garlic and fry until softened and lightly browned. Stir in the mushrooms and cook for 4–6 minutes until soft. Add the crème fraîche or soured cream and simmer for 2–3 minutes, then add the parsley, black pepper and chilli flakes.
3   Toss the pasta through the sauce, then serve in bowls.

Kidney Bean Curry

Kidney beans are known to be one of the richest sources of plant-based proteins and also contain a slow-releasing carbohydrate that takes longer to digest, so is beneficial for people with Type 2 diabetes. Kidney beans lend themselves to being teamed up with spices very well, including garam masala.

Note that it's crucial that you cook dried beans through completely, as undercooked kidney beans can prove toxic.

Serve the curry hot with a portion of basmati rice.

SERVES 4

400g tin kidney beans, drained and rinsed, or 200g dried kidney beans

3 tbsp extra virgin olive oil or sunflower oil

1 onion, finely chopped

4 garlic cloves, thinly sliced

Pinch of asafoetida (optional)

½ tsp ground cumin

½ tsp ground coriander

½ tsp ground turmeric

½ tsp chilli powder

1 tbsp tomato paste or purée

¼ tsp garam masala

1 tbsp peeled and grated root ginger or ginger paste

A few washed and chopped coriander leaves, to serve

1   If you're using dried kidney beans, rinse the beans and put
    them in a large bowl. Cover with cold water – the water
    should be three times the amount of beans (about 600ml) –
    and leave to soak overnight. The next day the water will have
    been absorbed by the beans and they will have doubled in
    size. Rinse or drain the beans three or four times until the
    water runs clear. Add the rinsed beans to a saucepan or pot
    and cover with clean water so the water sits at least 2.5cm
    above the beans. Bring to the boil, skimming off and
    discarding any froth that forms on the surface with a large
    spoon. Reduce the heat, cover and simmer for at least 1 hour
    15 minutes, or until the beans are soft. Drain and rinse.

2   Heat the oil in a saucepan over a medium heat, add the onion
    and garlic and fry for 7–9 minutes until the onion is
    caramelised, then add the asafoetida, if using, cumin,
    coriander, turmeric and chilli powder. Mix well, then stir in
    the tomato paste or purée. Add the tinned or cooked and
    drained kidney beans and cook over a low heat for 5–7
    minutes. Sprinkle over the garam masala and stir in the
    ginger. Garnish with the coriander leaves and serve.

Chana Aloo – Chickpeas with Potato

Kashmiri chilli powder is milder than traditional chilli powder and is often used in Indian dishes to create a vibrant colour with a hint of heat. Asafoetida is a pungent gum resin that is dried and then ground to a coarse yellowish powder. It is used to aid digestion and suppress feelings of bloatedness when consuming beans and pulses. Both are available in most Asian supermarkets in the spice section or online.

Serve this vegetable dish with wholemeal pitta breads.

SERVES 4

2 tbsp extra virgin olive oil or unsalted butter
1 bay leaf
½ tsp cumin seeds
1 onion, finely chopped
2 tsp peeled and grated root ginger or ginger paste
2–3 garlic cloves, finely chopped
½ tsp ground coriander
Pinch of Kashmiri chilli powder or chilli powder
½ tsp ground turmeric
¼ tsp freshly ground black pepper
1 tsp dried fenugreek leaves (optional)
Pinch of mango powder (amchoor) (optional)
Generous pinch of asafoetida (optional)
¼ tsp garam masala
200g tinned chopped tomatoes
400g tin chickpeas, drained and rinsed
2 floury potatoes (about 200g), peeled, boiled, and cut into
  2.5cm cubes
2 green chillies, split lengthways
A few washed and chopped coriander leaves

1   Heat the oil or butter in a heavy-based saucepan over a medium heat, then add the bay leaf and a few of the cumin seeds. Once they start to sizzle, add the remaining seeds. Tip in the onion, ginger and garlic and sauté until the mixture turns golden brown, then add the ground coriander, chilli powder, turmeric, black pepper, fenugreek, mango powder and asafoetida, if using, and garam masala. Sauté for a minute, then stir in the tomatoes and cook for 3–4 minutes until the mixture is well combined and thick. Add the chickpeas and the cooked potatoes with about 120ml of water, mix well, cover and simmer for 10 minutes, or until the flavours are combined.

2   Add the green chillies and the coriander leaves and serve.

Sun-dried Tomato Risotto

Sun-dried tomatoes have a particularly high concentration of lycopene, a powerful antioxidant that may help lower the risk of certain cancers, and are rich in fibre. Arborio rice is an Italian short-grain rice. When cooked, it becomes plump and soft in texture, with a chalky centre. The starch released from the rice during cooking gives the risotto its characteristic creaminess.

SERVES 2

1 tbsp extra virgin olive oil

1 onion, finely chopped

120g risotto or arborio rice

500ml warm vegetable stock (can be made from a low-sodium or low-salt stock cube, or see recipe on page 74)

75g pecorino or Cheddar cheese, grated

8–10 sun-dried tomatoes, chopped or sliced

¼ tsp freshly ground black pepper

1 tsp unsalted butter (optional)

1   Heat the oil in a saucepan over a medium heat and add the onion. Fry until golden brown, then add the rice and one-third of the warm stock. Cook for 5–7 minutes, stirring continuously, until the rice absorbs most of the stock, then add the remaining stock bit by bit, stirring all the time. When all the stock has been absorbed and the rice is cooked but still has a little bite, stir in the cheese and tomatoes and the pepper. Stir in the butter, if using, and serve hot.

Caper Puttanesca

Puttanesca is a classic Italian sauce made with garlic, olives, tomatoes, capers, and often anchovies. As tinned anchovies contain a considerable amount of salt, I've created a vegetarian version of the dish.

Capers add texture and tanginess to this dish with the wholewheat or wholegrain spaghetti giving a little more fibre than refined pasta.

SERVES 2

1 tsp extra virgin olive oil
2–3 garlic cloves, thinly sliced
200g tinned cherry tomatoes
1 tsp capers, drained
10–15 pitted black olives
¼ tsp freshly ground black pepper
100g wholewheat or wholegrain spaghetti
¼ tsp chilli flakes
A few basil leaves, washed

1   Heat the oil in a saucepan over a medium heat, add the garlic and cook for 2–3 minutes until it's beginning to turn lightly brown. Add the tomatoes, capers, olives and black pepper and simmer for 10 minutes until the sauce thickens.
2   Meanwhile, cook the spaghetti in fresh boiling water until it is tender but still al dente (firm to the bite). This should take about 10–12 minutes.
3   Using tongs, add the spaghetti to the pan with the sauce directly from the pasta cooking water, along with 2 tablespoons of the pasta cooking water, then mix together. Sprinkle with the chilli flakes and basil leaves and serve.

Egg and Cress Sandwich

Eggs are high in quality protein, which is needed to build, strengthen and repair the body and can also help you feel fuller for longer. This British classic is a perfect sandwich filler for a picnic or just to enjoy at home.

MAKES 2

2 medium free-range eggs
1 tsp Dijon or English mustard
1 tsp mayonnaise
1 punnet or 3 tbsp mustard cress
Generous pinch of ground white pepper
Pinch of sea salt (optional)
4 thin slices of rye, granary or wholemeal bread

1 Cook the eggs in a pan of boiling water for 8 minutes, then run them under a cold tap until they've cooled down. Remove the shells and set aside.

2 In a small bowl, mix together the mustard and mayonnaise. With a pair of clean scissors, chop the cress into the bowl. Add the cooked eggs and mash up the mixture with a fork. Season with the white pepper and the salt, if using.

3 Divide the mixture between two slices of the bread, then top with the remaining two slices. Cut the sandwiches into four quarters and serve.

Tomato and Thyme White Fish

White fish such as pollack or cod are a low-fat source of protein which makes them ideal for anyone wanting to reduce their fat intake and improve their heart health. Thyme is a herb that comes from the mint family and is known to help lower blood pressure. It also adds a lovely earthy flavour to the fish.

Serve with mashed potatoes and Green Beans with Lemon and Pepper Dressing (page 110).

SERVES 2

1 tbsp extra virgin olive oil
1 onion, finely chopped
200g tinned chopped tomatoes
¼ tsp freshly ground black pepper
A pinch of turmeric
½ tsp brown sugar
The leaves of a few sprigs of thyme, washed
2 pollack fillets, or any other white flaky fish, such as cod

1   Heat the oil in a frying pan over a medium heat, then add the onion and fry for 5–8 minutes until lightly browned. Add in the tomatoes, pepper, turmeric and sugar and mix, then add the thyme leaves and bring to the boil. Reduce the heat and simmer for 5 minutes. Put the fish into the sauce, cover and cook gently for 8–10 minutes until the fish flakes readily, then remove the frying pan from the heat and serve.

Puy Lentils in Chervil

Puy is a lentil grown in Le Puy, in the Auvergne region of France. It is deliciously nutty and lends itself well to cooking with spices and retains its shape. There's no need to soak puy lentils before cooking.

Lentils are packed with B vitamins, magnesium, zinc and potassium. Above all, they contain the plant compounds known as phytochemicals which protect against heart disease and Type 2 diabetes.

Serve with Parsley Rice (page 128).

SERVES 4

200g dried puy lentils
1 tbsp extra virgin olive oil
2 carrots, peeled and thinly sliced
2 garlic cloves, crushed, or 2 tsp garlic purée
Pinch of sea salt (optional)
Freshly ground white pepper, to taste
300ml vegetable stock (can be made from a low-sodium or low-salt stock cube, or see recipe on page 74)
Handful of fresh chervil leaves, washed and finely chopped

1   Put the lentils in a small saucepan and cover with twice their depth in water. Bring to the boil, then reduce the heat and simmer for 15–20 minutes until tender, skimming away any foam that rises to the surface. Top up the water if you need to. Drain the lentils, then tip into a large bowl.

2   Heat the olive oil in a saucepan over a medium heat, add the carrots and garlic and sweat until soft. Add the sea salt, if using, and the pepper and cook for 2–3 minutes, then stir in the drained lentils, add the stock and bring to the boil. Cook for 10–12 minutes, until thickened, add the chervil and mix, then serve.

Broccoli Bake

This dish adds extra appeal to popular broccoli, with the green chilli giving heat and oomph.

Broccoli is loaded with the antioxidant vitamins C and B, which are required for maintaining good immune and nervous system health. Broccoli also aids detoxification and cleansing of the liver.

SERVES 2
200g broccoli florets
100ml semi-skimmed milk
1 tbsp plain flour
100g Cheddar cheese, grated
1 garlic clove, finely chopped
Pinch of grated nutmeg
Slice of stale bread, torn into small pieces
1/4 tsp freshly ground black pepper
1 green chilli, finely chopped (optional)
1 tbsp extra virgin olive oil

1 Preheat the oven to 180°C/350°F/Gas 4.
2 Cook the broccoli florets in a saucepan of boiling water for 5–7 minutes until a little tender. If you prefer, you could steam the broccoli to help retain its nutrients. Drain and place in an ovenproof casserole dish.
3 Pour the milk into a saucepan and bring to the boil over a medium heat, then add the flour, whisking continuously, followed by three-quarters of the cheese. Add the garlic and nutmeg and continue stirring for 2–3 minutes until fairly smooth and slightly thickened.
4 Pour the sauce over the broccoli, then scatter the bread pieces on top. Sprinkle over the remaining cheese, black pepper and chilli, if using. Drizzle the olive oil over the top of the bread pieces to make them crispy, or brush the oil on the bread using a pastry brush. Bake in the oven for 20–25 minutes, until golden brown on top. Serve immediately.

Salmon with Ginger and Chilli Dressing

Salmon is a nutritious fish, rich in omega 3 fatty acids. Omega 3 fats are a group of unsaturated fats that are particularly beneficial for good heart health. In places where people eat more oily fish, such as in the Mediterranean, Greenland and Japan, fewer people have heart disease, compared to countries where people eat very little oily fish, such as the UK.

This recipe uses microwaveable rice, a convenient shortcut, but if you prefer to cook brown basmati rice from scratch, you will need 200g of dried rice and 625ml water. Keep an eye on the water level as the rice cooks and top it up if necessary.

SERVES 2

2 salmon fillets (about 240g each)
3 heads of pak choi or bok choy, washed, trimmed
  and halved lengthways
250g microwaveable brown basmati or wholegrain rice packet

For the dressing
2 tbsp low-sodium (low-salt) soy sauce
Juice of 1 lime
2 tsp peeled and grated root ginger or ginger paste
$\frac{1}{4}$ tsp freshly ground black pepper
$\frac{1}{2}$ red chilli, chopped, or a few chilli flakes
2 spring onions, washed and finely chopped
A few washed and chopped coriander leaves
Pinch of brown sugar

1   Half-fill a saucepan with water and bring to the boil. Put the
    salmon fillets in a steamer or a colander and top with the pak
    choi. Place the colander or steamer over the saucepan of
    boiling water. Seal firmly with a lid or some foil and steam
    for 8–10 minutes, or until the salmon is cooked through.

2   Meanwhile, microwave the rice according to the
    instructions on the packet.

3   Combine the soy sauce, lime juice, ginger, pepper, chilli or
    chilli flakes, spring onions, coriander and sugar together in a
    small bowl and set aside.

4   Portion out the pak choi, salmon fillets and rice between two
    shallow bowls and pour the dressing over the top. Serve
    immediately.

Seafood Spaghetti

The inspiration for this dish is the sunny climes of the Mediterranean and eating alfresco while watching the world go by.

Any kind of pasta is high in carbohydrates, which could be bad for you if consumed in large amounts. Traditionally made from durum wheat and water or eggs, it is turned into different shapes and then cooked in boiling water. Wholegrain or wholewheat pasta contains all parts of the wheat kernel, which contains many nutrients and is high in fibre. If you find the wholegrain pasta too heavy, cook some of each of the two types – refined and wholegrain – separately and then serve them together.

SERVES 4

1 tbsp extra virgin olive oil
1 onion, finely chopped
2 garlic cloves, finely chopped
1 tsp sweet smoked paprika
¼ tsp freshly ground black pepper
¼ tsp chilli flakes (optional)
400g tin chopped tomatoes
1 low-sodium or low-salt fish or vegetable stock cube
240g pack of frozen cooked seafood mix, defrosted
300g wholegrain or wholewheat spaghetti, roughly broken
Handful of flat-leaf parsley leaves, washed and chopped
1 lemon, cut into wedges

1   Heat the oil in a wok or large frying pan over a medium heat,
    add the onion and garlic and cook for 5 minutes until soft.
    Add the paprika, black pepper and the chilli flakes, if using,
    and cook for a minute, then tip in the tomatoes and continue
    to cook for 5–6 minutes until the mixture thickens. Crumble
    in the stock cube, add the defrosted seafood mix and cook for
    a further 4–5 minutes.

2   Cook the spaghetti in fresh boiling water until it is tender
    but still al dente (firm to the bite). This should take about 10
    minutes. Drain the spaghetti and run under a cold tap.

3   Add the pasta to the seafood and reduce the heat. Stir the
    mixture and cook for 5–6 minutes, stirring occasionally to
    stop the pasta from sticking. Sprinkle with parsley and serve
    with the lemon wedges.

Pesto-crusted Cod Fillet

The walnut pesto gives the baked fish a nice crunch along with the citrus flavour in this simple dish.

Cod, like many fish, is a good source of omega 3 fatty acids that the body cannot produce but needs in order to help lower triglycerides, a type of unhealthy cholesterol. Eating fish like cod at least once a week can also help reduce the risk of heart disease and stroke.

Serve this dish with Tartare Sauce (page 120) and Broccoli Bake (page 59).

SERVES 2

2 tbsp pesto (Walnut Pesto opposite or shop-bought pesto)
50g breadcrumbs
¼ tsp freshly ground black pepper
A few flat-leaf parsley leaves, washed and finely chopped
Grated zest of 1 unwaxed lemon, plus a few wedges, to serve
2 cod or pollack fillets with skin (about 200g each)

1   Combine the pesto, breadcrumbs, black pepper, parsley and lemon zest in a bowl and mix well. Preheat the oven to 180°C/350°F/Gas 4.
2   Place the cod fillets on a roasting tray, skin side down. Spread half of the pesto over each fillet. Bake in the oven for 15–17 minutes until the cod is cooked, then serve.

Walnut Pesto

Walnuts provide fibre, vitamins and minerals, and are a good source of the plant-based omega 3 fatty acids, which may help reduce the risk of heart disease. They also contain other plant compounds that can help decrease inflammation, which is a key offender in many chronic illnesses.

MAKES ABOUT 10 SMALL PORTIONS
40g walnuts
2 garlic cloves, roughly chopped
80g fresh basil leaves, washed
¼ tsp fresh ground black pepper
Pinch of sea salt (optional)
100ml extra virgin olive oil
30g pecorino cheese or Cheddar cheese, grated

1   Place the walnuts and garlic in the bowl of a food processor fitted with a steel blade and process for about 10 seconds until coarsely chopped. Add the basil leaves, pepper and salt, if using, and process for a minute until the mixture forms a paste. Pour in the olive oil and process again until the pesto is thoroughly blended. Add the cheese and process for a minute more.

2   Use the pesto immediately or store it in the fridge in a tightly sealed jar or airtight container covered with a thin layer of olive oil. This seals it from the air and prevents the pesto from oxidising, which would make it turn brown in colour. It will keep in the fridge for about a week. Pesto can be frozen in an airtight container for up to 6 months. You can also divide your prepared pesto into the compartments of an ice cube tray and freeze. Remove the pesto cubes from the tray and put in a sealable plastic bag or airtight container. You can add the defrosted pesto cubes to soups, pasta dishes or serve as a side relish.

Chinese-style Fried Rice

This medley of vegetables in one dish contains different combinations of vitamins, minerals, fibre and other nutrients. In order to gain their maximum benefits, try not to overcook the vegetables.

Refrigerated cooked rice can be used in this recipe if you like, because when rice is chilled, the grains don't tend to stick together. This makes it the perfect consistency. But remember to only reheat rice once.

SERVES 2

80g brown or white long-grain rice, such as basmati, washed

2 tbsp low-sodium (low-salt) soy sauce

2 free-range eggs, beaten

2 tbsp sunflower oil

3–4 garlic cloves, thinly sliced

2 tsp peeled and grated root ginger or ginger paste

1 green chilli, chopped

1 carrot, peeled, washed and cut lengthways into thin strips

3 tbsp frozen peas or petits pois, thawed

2 spring onions, washed and chopped

1 tsp toasted sesame oil

¼ tsp chilli flakes (optional)

¼–½ tsp ground white pepper or Chinese five-spice powder

- **To cook brown rice**, place it in a saucepan, add 475ml freshly boiled water, and cook for 45 minutes–1 hour, until the water has been absorbed and the rice is tender. Set aside.
- **To cook white rice**, put the rice in a saucepan with 120ml water and bring to the boil. Reduce the heat, cover and cook for 8–10 minutes until all the water has been absorbed.

1   Add a teaspoon of the soy sauce to the beaten eggs and mix. Heat 1 tablespoon of the sunflower oil in a frying pan or wok over a medium heat, tip in the beaten eggs and cook for 2 minutes, then – using a slotted spoon – flip it over and cook the other side. Remove the omelette from the pan and cut it into thin strips. Set aside.

2   Heat the remaining sunflower oil in the wok or frying pan over a medium heat, tip in the garlic, ginger and green chilli and stir-fry until well mixed. Add the carrot strips, peas and spring onions and sauté for a minute. Tip in the cooked rice and mix thoroughly. Add the remaining soy sauce and sesame oil and season with chilli flakes, if using, and white pepper or Chinese five-spice powder. Toss it all together and remove from the heat. Spoon the rice into individual serving plates and garnish with the strips of omelette.

Open Tuna Baps

Tuna is a good source of protein and B vitamins such as niacin, which benefits the skin and the nervous system. Do bear in mind that tinned tuna may contain more salt than fresh.

SERVES 2

1 red onion, finely chopped, or a few chives, washed and finely snipped

2 tbsp sweetcorn kernels (drained if tinned)

200g tinned, drained tuna chunks (in water)

1 tomato, washed and finely chopped

¼ tsp ground white pepper

2 wholemeal baps, halved

150g Cheddar cheese, grated

A few pitted green olives, sliced into rings (optional)

For the dressing

2 tbsp extra virgin olive oil

Juice of ½ lemon

1 tsp Dijon mustard

To serve

A few lettuce (or other salad) leaves, washed and sliced

¼ cucumber, washed and peeled into thin ribbons

1 Preheat the grill to medium.
2 In a mixing bowl, combine the onion or chives, sweetcorn, tuna, tomato and pepper. With a spoon, place enough of the tuna mixture onto the cut sides of the baps to cover the bread generously, spreading the filling evenly. Sprinkle the grated cheese on top and scatter with the olives, if using. Put the baps on a baking tray under the hot grill for 2–3 minutes until the cheese has melted and is slightly bubbling.
3 Whisk the dressing ingredients together with a fork and drizzle over the leaves and cucumber. Serve with the grilled tuna baps.

Turmeric and Mushroom Rice

This recipe can be prepared using white rice, but brown rice gives a nuttier flavour and is rich in dietary fibre. Do bear in mind that white rice cooks more quickly than brown rice. You could replace the mushrooms with frozen vegetables such as peas and carrots (some frozen veg won't need 35–40 minutes cooking time, so can be added to the pan later in the cooking process).

SERVES 3-4

1 tbsp extra virgin olive oil
½ onion, chopped
100g mushrooms, wiped clean and sliced
1 garlic clove, crushed, or 1 tsp garlic purée
½ tsp ground turmeric
¼ tsp freshly ground black pepper
Pinch of sea salt
200g brown rice, washed
A few curly-leaf parsley leaves, washed and chopped

1   Heat the oil in a saucepan over a medium heat, add the onion and sauté for 3–4 minutes until softened. Add the mushrooms and stir-fry for 3–4 minutes, then tip in the garlic and sauté for a further couple of minutes. Stir in the turmeric, black pepper and salt.

2   Add the rice and mix well to combine all the ingredients. Pour in 625ml water, bring to the boil and cook over a medium heat for 35–40 minutes, stirring occasionally, until all of the water has been absorbed by the rice. Check that the rice is tender. If the rice is not yet cooked, add 3–4 more tablespoons of water and cook for another 5–7 minutes. When cooked, add the parsley and stir. Serve hot.

Brown Rice with Brown Lentils – Mujadara

Lentils are high in protein and fibre. Unlike dried beans, lentils don't need to be soaked before cooking. This recipe is a Middle Eastern lentil- and rice-based dish. Bulgur wheat can be used instead of rice, if you prefer (it will cook more quickly).

SERVES 4

100g brown lentils
2 tbsp extra virgin olive oil
1 onion, thinly sliced
100g brown basmati rice, washed
½ tsp ground cumin
½ tsp ground allspice
¼ tsp ground coriander
¼ tsp ground cinnamon
Seeds of 2–3 green cardamom pods, ground

1　Put the lentils in a saucepan and add water until the water level is 3–4cm above the lentils. Bring the water to the boil, then reduce the heat and cook for 30–40 minutes until the lentils are tender. They should hold their shape, but be soft when pressed. Remove from the heat and set aside.

2　While the lentils are cooking, heat the oil in a saucepan over a medium heat, add the onion and sauté for 6–7 minutes until golden brown. Remove the onion from the pan using a slotted spoon, leaving the oil in the pan. Add the rice and the spices to the pan and sauté, stirring, for a minute. Add water until the water level is 1–2cm above the rice. Bring to the boil then reduce the heat, cover and cook for 30–40 minutes over a medium-low heat until the rice absorbs all the water and is tender. Mix in the cooked lentils and cook, covered, for 2 minutes, then remove from the heat and fluff the rice and lentils with a fork.

3　Serve topped with the caramelised onion.

Fish in a Light Coconut Curry

Mustard seeds are an excellent source of selenium, which helps to decrease some of the symptoms associated with rheumatoid arthritis, and are also rich in magnesium, which is known to reduce the incidence of migraine attacks. Mustard seeds also add a lovely nutty flavour to curries and snacks.

Serve with brown rice.

SERVES 4

2 tbsp groundnut or sunflower oil
1 tsp brown or black mustard seeds
A few curry leaves (optional)
1 onion, finely chopped
4 garlic cloves, finely chopped
2 green chillies, finely chopped
½ tsp ground turmeric
1 tsp ground coriander
1 tsp ground cumin
¼ tsp sea salt (optional)
4 tbsp coconut milk
800g skinless white fish fillets, such as coley, pollack or cod, cut into 4cm chunks

1   Heat the oil in a saucepan over a medium heat, add a few of the mustard seeds, and when they start to crackle, add the remaining seeds and stir. Mix in the curry leaves, if using, then tip in the onion and fry for 4–5 minutes until softened. Stir in the garlic and chillies and sauté for another minute, then add the turmeric, coriander, cumin and salt, if using, and mix well. Add 2 tablespoons of the coconut milk along with 100ml of water and mix, then add the fish pieces and simmer gently for 5–6 minutes. Mix in the remaining 2 tablespoons of the coconut milk and cook for another minute, check that the fish is cooked through, then serve.

Soups

....

Soups are a great way to stay feeling full and can give your immune system a boost. They could also help you ward off colds and flu with their disease-fighting nutrients.

Cost effective and easy to prepare, soups require very little skill. They can be made in advance and can freeze well, too (defrost thoroughly before reheating). As they're mostly liquid, they keep you hydrated during the winter months when it's not uncommon to drink less than you need – although you may not be feeling hot and sweaty, you still lose fluid through everyday activities. Soups are also warming when temperatures drop, especially when you add ingredients such as ginger, chilli, cloves and cinnamon. All in all, these one-pot wonders can uplift your mood and sense of wellbeing.

Vegetable Stock

Making your own stock not only ensures that you know what has gone into it, but also makes your dishes taste better and it's more nutritious than powdered or cubed stock, too. Just a little preparation results in a thrifty yet additive- and salt-free stock that can be made ahead and used in soups, stews and curries. You can add a cinnamon stick to boost the spiciness if you like.

Feel free to use up vegetable odds and ends from your fridge drawer in this, just wash them thoroughly first.

MAKES 1–1.5 LITRES

1 tbsp extra virgin olive oil
2–3 bay leaves
3–4 spring onions or 1 onion, washed and roughly chopped
2 fennel bulbs and fennel tops, washed and roughly chopped (optional)
1 carrot, washed and chopped
1 parsnip, washed and chopped
2 celery sticks and celery leaves, washed and roughly chopped
2 garlic cloves, gently crushed
2.5cm piece root ginger, washed
20 black peppercorns
Sprig of rosemary, washed

1   Heat a stock pot or a large saucepan over a medium heat and add the oil. Add the bay leaves and stir, then add the spring onions or onion, fennel and fennel tops, if using, carrot, parsnip, celery and celery leaves and sweat for 2–3 minutes. Pour in enough cold water to generously cover the vegetables and increase the heat to high. Add the garlic, ginger, peppercorns and rosemary sprig and stir. Bring to the boil and simmer for 15 minutes.
2   Pour the stock through a sieve. Discard the vegetable pieces or reserve for another use. The liquid stock is ready to be used.
3   The stock can be stored in the fridge for up to 3 days, or frozen in ice-cube trays for up to 4 months.

Clear and Spiced Chicken Soup

If you're recovering from an illness or feeling a bit run down, this soup is nourishing, easy to eat and comforting. It is often prepared in Indian households to treat colds, coughs and flu. The ginger and garlic soothe the throat, while the cloves and peppercorns add warmth.

If you have any roast chicken leftover from a meal, freeze it in a suitable bag, then defrost thoroughly for use in this dish.

SERVES 2

1 roast chicken carcass or leftover pieces of roast chicken
A few slices of onion
1 garlic clove
2.5cm piece root ginger
1 tsp butter
2cm piece cinnamon stick
2 cloves
2–4 black peppercorns
¼ tsp ground turmeric
A few washed and chopped coriander leaves, to serve

1   Put the chicken, onion, garlic and ginger into a saucepan with 500ml water. Bring to the boil and let it boil for 15 minutes, then turn off the heat and strain the stock into a bowl. Discard the bones, onion and flavourings.

2   Take another saucepan, or wash the one in which you made the stock and place it over a medium heat. Add the butter, cinnamon, cloves, black peppercorns and turmeric and fry for 1 minute, then pour in the stock and mix. Serve hot in a mug or soup bowl, garnished with the coriander leaves.

Herby Pumpkin Soup

Packed with beta-carotene, which is great for eye health, this recipe uses the pumpkin's orange flesh to make a deliciously creamy soup that can be cooked and frozen in batches. You could use frozen chunks of pumpkin and dried herbs to make the preparation easier, if you like.

SERVES 4

2 tbsp extra virgin olive oil

2 onions, finely chopped

5 garlic cloves, chopped

1.5–2kg pumpkin, peeled, deseeded and chopped into chunks

½ tsp ground white or black pepper

A few sprigs of thyme, washed and leaves picked

Sprig of rosemary, washed and needles picked

1.5 litres vegetable stock (can be made from 2 low-sodium or low-salt stock cubes, or see recipe on page 74)

1   Heat the olive oil in a large saucepan over a medium heat, then add the onions and cook gently for 5 minutes, until softened. Add the garlic and sauté for another 3–4 minutes, then add the pumpkin and cook for a further 12–15 minutes, stirring occasionally, until it starts to soften and turn golden. Tip in the white or black pepper, followed by the thyme and rosemary and mix well. Pour in the stock, bring to the boil and simmer for 10 minutes until the pumpkin is very soft.

2   Purée the soup with a stick blender. If you find the soup is too thick, add a little more water to bring it to the required consistency. Serve.

3   This soup can be frozen in an airtight container for up to 2 months. Defrost thoroughly before reheating.

Lebanese Lentil Soup

Red lentils are split, cook quickly and don't need to be soaked. They have a nutty, sweet flavour and are great for making Indian dal dishes. In this recipe, the lentils are simmered with chicken stock and seasonings, then puréed until smooth, before being served with coriander and lemon juice. It's a hearty soup, packed full of protein and flavour.

SERVES 4

1.5 litres chicken stock (can be made from 2 low-sodium or low-salt stock cubes)
150g red lentils
3 tbsp extra virgin olive oil
4 garlic cloves, chopped
1 large onion, chopped
1 tbsp ground cumin
½ tsp cayenne pepper
Handful of washed and chopped coriander leaves
1 tbsp lemon juice

1   Bring the chicken stock and lentils to the boil in a large saucepan over a high heat, then reduce the heat to medium-low. Cover and simmer for 20 minutes.
2   Meanwhile, heat the olive oil in a frying pan over a medium heat, add the garlic and onion and cook, stirring, for 3 minutes, until softened. Remove from the heat.
3   Stir the onion mixture into the lentils and season with the cumin and cayenne.
4   Continue simmering for about 10 minutes until the lentils are tender, then remove from the heat and carefully purée the soup in a liquidiser or with a stick blender until smooth. Stir in the coriander leaves and lemon juice before serving.
5   This soup can be frozen in an airtight container for up to 3 months. Defrost thoroughly before reheating.

Pea Soup – Potage St Germain

The colour of this soup is incredibly vibrant and the shallots add a greater depth of flavour to the dish.

Peas belong to the group of foods known as legumes, which are plants that produce pods with seeds or beans inside such as lentils, soy beans, chickpeas and all types of beans. Peas are packed with antioxidants that help maintain your immune system, as well as anti-inflammatory nutrients associated with lowering the risk of diabetes, heart disease and arthritis.

SERVES 4

40g unsalted butter

2–3 shallots, chopped

400g shelled peas or frozen petits pois

½ tsp caster or granulated sugar

½ tsp ground white pepper

1 litre vegetable stock (can be made from 2 low-sodium or low-salt stock cubes, or see recipe on page 74)

1 Melt the butter in a large saucepan over a medium heat, add the shallots and fry, stirring, for 2–3 minutes until softened. Add the peas, sugar and pepper and sauté for 7–8 minutes, then add 120ml water and cook for a further 2 minutes. Remove from the heat and allow to cool.

2 Blend the peas in the pan using a stick blender and put the puréed mixture back on the hob over a low heat. Add the vegetable stock and simmer for about 10 minutes, then gradually stir the soup until it has a smooth and soup-like consistency. Serve immediately.

3 This soup can be frozen in an airtight container for up to 3 months. Defrost thoroughly before reheating.

Mushroom Soup

Fresh garlic lifts the flavour of common chestnut or button mushrooms to give this soup a luxurious texture and taste.

Mushrooms are rich in B vitamins that have a direct impact on energy levels, brain function and cell metabolism.

SERVES 4

2 tbsp extra virgin olive oil

2 onions, roughly chopped

4 garlic cloves, roughly chopped

250g mushrooms, wiped clean and thinly sliced

¼ tsp ground white pepper

1 litre vegetable stock (can be made from 2 low-sodium or low-salt stock cubes, or see recipe on page 74)

50g croutons (optional), to serve

1   Heat the oil in a saucepan over a medium heat, add the onion and sauté gently for 3 minutes, then add the garlic and sauté for another minute. Add the mushrooms and cook the mixture for 5–6 minutes until the mushrooms soften and any excess liquid from the mushrooms has evaporated. Stir in the pepper and the vegetable stock, bring to the boil and simmer for 15–20 minutes until the mixture has thickened slightly and reached a soupy consistency.

2   Blitz the soup with a stick blender or liquidiser until smooth, then serve, scattered with a few croutons, if using.

3   This soup can be frozen in an airtight container for up to 3 months. Defrost thoroughly before reheating.

Mexican-style Pepper Soup

Celery helps carry away toxins from the body, thus keeping skin looking fresh and revitalised, and red peppers are a rich source of vitamin C that fights cell damage. The medium-sweet ancho chilli in this recipe adds a delicious Mexican flavour to the soup.

SERVES 4

1 dried ancho chilli (or any dried chilli, or a generous pinch of chilli flakes)

2 tbsp extra virgin olive oil

1 onion, finely chopped

2 celery sticks, washed and finely chopped

3–4 garlic cloves, finely chopped

2 tsp sweet smoked paprika

2 tsp ground cumin

4 roasted red peppers, from a jar, chopped

1 litre vegetable stock (can be made from 2 low-sodium or low-salt stock cubes, or see recipe on page 74)

Juice of 1 lime

To serve

Handful of coriander leaves, washed and chopped

1 lime, cut into wedges

1 If using the dried chilli, put the chilli into a small heatproof bowl and pour in enough boiling water to cover it. Leave for 10 minutes, then drain. When cool enough to handle, remove the stalk.

2 Heat the oil in a saucepan over a medium heat, add the onion and celery and cook for about 10 minutes until softened, then add the garlic and cook for another minute. Tip in the paprika and cumin and cook for another minute, until you can smell the aroma of the spices. Add the soaked chilli or chilli flakes, red peppers and stock and simmer for 15 minutes. Remove from the heat and use a stick blender to whizz until smooth. Stir the lime juice into the soup and serve, garnished with the coriander, with lime wedges alongside.

3 This soup can be frozen in an airtight container (minus the lime wedges and the coriander leaves) for up to 3 months. Defrost thoroughly before reheating.

Pizza Soup

This soup has the flavours of a pizza in a bowl. It can also be used as a sauce for a pasta dish. Make sure you get hold of garlic granules or powder and not garlic salt, which is often more salt than garlic.

Peppers are packed with fibre and vitamins A and C. The red variety of peppers have more beta-carotene and vitamin C than the green ones, and are sweeter.

SERVES 6

2 tbsp extra virgin olive oil

1 onion, finely chopped

3–4 garlic cloves, finely chopped

1 tbsp tomato purée

400g tin chopped tomatoes

300g frozen mixed vegetables, such as peppers, mushrooms and sweetcorn

1 tsp garlic granules or garlic powder

¼ tsp freshly ground black pepper

1 tbsp dried mixed herbs

Generous pinch of dried oregano

1 tbsp balsamic vinegar

2 tsp caster or granulated sugar (optional)

350ml vegetable stock (can be made from a low-sodium or low-salt stock cube, or see recipe on page 74)

To serve

Grated mozzarella (optional)

A few basil leaves, washed and chopped

6 tbsp croutons

1   Heat the oil in a saucepan over a medium heat, add the onion
    and garlic and cook gently until softened, then stir in the
    tomato purée and mix well. Tip in the tomatoes and cook for
    a few minutes until the mixture is quite thick, then add the
    vegetables and cook for 3–4 minutes until the vegetables are
    coated with the sauce. Stir in the garlic granules or powder,
    black pepper, mixed herbs and oregano. Stir, then add the
    balsamic vinegar and sugar, if using. Pour in the stock, stir,
    bring to a simmer and cook for 10–15 minutes until the
    vegetables are tender.

2   This soup can be left chunky or blended in a food processor
    or with a stick blender until smooth.

3   Garnish with the grated mozzarella, if using, and the basil
    leaves and croutons.

4   This soup can be frozen in an airtight container (minus the
    mozzarella, basil and croutons) for up to 3 months. Defrost
    thoroughly before reheating.

Salads

Salads are easy to make at home and require no cooking. Eating a daily portion of leafy greens can be one of the best habits to get into, be it in summer or winter. Besides what they offer in flavour, crunchy textures, colours and aromas, consuming a large serving of fresh raw vegetables each day can have significant health benefits. A diet rich in vegetables and fruits can lower blood pressure, reduce the risk of heart disease and stroke, help prevent some types of cancer, lower the risk of eye and digestive problems, and have a positive effect on blood sugar levels, which can help keep appetite in check. They are a natural source of fibre, too.

You can add an extra dimension to your salads by making your own salad dressings with a flavour boost from herbs, including basil, parsley, thyme, coriander, dill, rosemary and fresh oregano, or garlic, lemon and even fresh chilli.

Iceberg Salad

Although it's low in fibre, iceberg lettuce has a high water content and does offer some nutritional benefits. Iceberg can be part of a balanced diet and improve gut health. Combine iceberg with other vegetables and greens such as in this salad.

This salad is my favourite allrounder.

SERVES 4

1 small iceberg lettuce
Handful of dill, washed and roughly chopped
Handful of coriander leaves, washed and chopped
1 shallot or red onion, finely chopped

For the dressing
4 tbsp white wine vinegar
¼ tsp caster sugar
2 tbsp extra virgin olive oil
Grated zest and juice of 1 unwaxed lemon
½ tsp ground white pepper
½ tsp English mustard powder or Dijon mustard

1 Wash the lettuce under a cold tap and place in a colander to drain. Pat the lettuce dry. Remove the outer leaves (which could be wilted or dirty), cut out the core and chop the remaining lettuce into 4cm pieces. Place in a salad bowl.
2 For the dressing, place the ingredients in a screw-top jar. Screw a lid on and shake for a few seconds until the mixture is well combined.
3 Mix the dill, coriander and shallot or onion together in a bowl and drizzle a third of the dressing over them about 20 minutes before serving the salad.
4 Just before serving the salad, pour the remaining dressing from the jar over the lettuce leaves, add the dill, coriander and shallot or onion mixture, and serve.

Portuguese Salad

Red cabbage is full of fibre and a good mix of vitamins and minerals known to lower inflammation. It's very versatile and can be eaten raw or cooked. This salad is also great as an accompaniment to other main dishes.

SERVES 4
2 tbsp extra virgin olive oil
250g red cabbage, cut into thin strips and washed
Pinch of sea salt
¼ tsp freshly ground black pepper
1 tbsp balsamic vinegar

1 Heat the oil in a saucepan over a medium heat, tip in the cabbage and cook for 5–6 minutes until softened (you don't want it to lose too much of its shape or texture). Season with the salt, pepper and balsamic vinegar and cook for a further 2 minutes until the cabbage is well cooked, adding a little water if necessary. Serve hot or warm.

Lebanese Salad

Baharat is a Middle Eastern spice blend used to flavour meat, fish and vegetables. It's a combination of coriander, cardamom, cumin and paprika and other warming spices such as cloves, peppercorns, cinnamon and nutmeg. See page 132 for the spice blend recipe.

SERVES 2

1 romaine lettuce, leaves washed and torn
4 tomatoes, washed and roughly chopped
1 small red onion, thinly sliced
1 medium carrot, peeled, washed and grated
¼ cucumber, washed and thinly sliced
10 pitted black or green olives, thinly sliced

For the dressing
1 tbsp extra virgin olive oil
1 tbsp lemon juice
1 tsp pomegranate molasses
1 tsp runny honey
Pinch of baharat spice blend (page 132)
1 garlic clove, crushed, or 1 tsp garlic purée

1 Place all the salad ingredients in a bowl.
2 Whisk the dressing ingredients in a small bowl or put them into a screw-top jar, seal with the lid and shake.
3 Just before serving the salad, drizzle the dressing over the salad ingredients in the bowl.

Warm Chicken Salad

This combination of ingredients makes a refreshing change from eating mundane sandwiches. Balsamic vinegar, which is used in many dressings, has a bold and tart flavour, and can help block toxic cells in the body that can raise cholesterol levels.

SERVES 2

2 skinless chicken breasts, or 2 roasted chicken breasts or 250g cooked chicken slices, cut into bite-sized pieces

½ small baguette (ideally wholemeal), cut into bite-sized pieces

3 tbsp extra virgin olive oil

1 tbsp balsamic vinegar

1 tsp runny honey

Pinch of freshly ground black pepper

150g bag of mixed salad leaves, washed

250g pack of cooked beetroot (not in vinegar), cut into bite-sized pieces

100g goat's cheese or Cheddar cheese, cut into 2cm cubes

1 Preheat the oven to 180°C/350°F/Gas 4.

2 Spread the chicken pieces (if using pre-cooked chicken) and baguette pieces out in a shallow roasting tray. Drizzle with 2 tablespoons of the olive oil and toss to coat. Bake in the oven for 15 minutes until the chicken is cooked through and the bread is golden and crisp. If you are using cooked chicken, add it to the roasting tray for the last 5 minutes, to warm it through.

3 Whisk together the remaining 1 tablespoon of olive oil with the balsamic vinegar, the honey and pepper.

4 Divide the salad leaves between two serving plates, add the beetroot, then scatter the cheese over. Toss with the warm chicken and bread. Drizzle with the dressing just before serving.

Lockdown Salad

This salad made with store-cupboard ingredients can be eaten any time of day.

The tuna adds to the protein content of this salad and is low in fat. Dill is a good source of vitamin C and elevates the flavour of this salad.

SERVES 2

2 x 160g tins tuna (in water), drained

1 tomato, washed and roughly chopped

1 green or red chilli, finely chopped (optional)

4–5 pitted olives, roughly chopped (optional)

½ red onion, chopped (save the other half for another recipe – you can freeze them)

1 tbsp lemon juice

¼ tsp ground white or black pepper

3 tbsp mayonnaise

A few washed and chopped dill fronds

1 Place the tuna in a bowl and flake it a little. Add the tomato, the chilli and olives, if using, add the onion and mix.

2 Just before serving, stir in the lemon juice and pepper and fold in the mayonnaise. Garnish with the dill and serve.

Coronation Turkey Salad

Turkey's not just for festive occasions – it can be part of a healthy everyday meal plan, too. Turkey meat is a nutritious, low-fat source of protein that is rich in zinc and selenium, and helps to repair cell DNA and lower the risk of cancer. You could replace the turkey with chicken if you like, which is also packed with vitamins B3 and B6 that support skin health and may help prevent anaemia and tiredness.

SERVES 4

2 tbsp sunflower oil
1 tsp Madras curry paste or ½ tsp Madras curry powder
400g leftover or shop-bought roast turkey, cut into
   bite-sized pieces
2 tbsp mango chutney
1 tbsp mayonnaise
2 tsp double cream (optional)
Dash of lemon juice
Pinch of freshly ground black pepper
¼ cucumber, washed and finely chopped or sliced
A few sprigs of watercress or iceberg lettuce leaves, washed
1 tbsp flaked almonds (optional)
½ loaf crusty baguette, thickly sliced

1   Heat 1 tablespoon of the oil in a frying pan over a medium heat, add the curry paste or powder and stir for a few seconds. Toss in the turkey and fry for 5–6 minutes to warm it through and brown it lightly.

2   In a large bowl, whisk together the remaining oil with the mango chutney, mayonnaise and cream, if using. Add the lemon juice and black pepper and mix well.

3   Toss in the cucumber, watercress or lettuce, the turkey and half of the flaked almonds, if using. Scatter with the rest of the almonds and serve with the crusty bread on the side.

Green Salad with Vinaigrette

A vinaigrette is a dressing to drizzle over salads. It is made with a little oil and an acidic ingredient such as lemon juice or vinegar, and herbs and spices can be added to enhance the flavour. Shop-bought vinaigrettes may contain large quantities of salt and sugar, so it's worthwhile making your own. Once you start making homemade vinaigrettes, you won't go back to using shop-bought!

SERVES 2

2 tsp Dijon mustard
2 tbsp red wine vinegar or balsamic vinegar
1 tsp runny honey
6 tbsp olive oil
Pinch of freshly ground black pepper
2 large handfuls of green salad leaves, washed

1 Put the mustard, vinegar, honey and olive oil in a screw-top jar and season with the black pepper. Seal with the lid and shake vigorously to mix.
2 Place the salad leaves in a bowl and add the vinaigrette just before serving.
3 The dressing can be stored in a cool place (not the fridge) for up to a week.

Spiced Mango and Cucumber Salad

What I like about this salad is the vibrant colours and the exotic taste you get when the ingredients are combined.

Even a tiny amount of chilli contains high levels of the anti-viral antioxidant beta-carotene. Remember that most of the spicy heat of the chilli is contained in the white membranes of the chilli and not the seeds.

SERVES 2

¼ cucumber, washed and cut into small pieces
½ small red onion, finely chopped
1 garlic clove, crushed or finely chopped, or 1 tsp garlic purée (optional)
1 tsp groundnut or sunflower oil
2 tomatoes, washed and finely chopped
1 red chilli or 2 green jalapeño chillies, finely chopped
¼ tsp ground cumin
Pinch of ground cinnamon
1 ripe mango, peeled, pitted and roughly chopped
1 tbsp dry-roasted peanuts, coarsely crushed (optional)
1 tbsp washed and roughly chopped coriander leaves
1 tbsp lime juice

1   Mix the cucumber in a bowl with the onion and garlic, if using.
2   Toss together the oil, tomatoes, red chilli or jalapeños, cumin, cinnamon and mango in a large bowl. Add the cucumber mixture to the bowl and toss to combine. Sprinkle the peanuts over, if using, and finish with the coriander and lime juice.

Italian-style Tuna and Bean Salad

Cannellini beans, when cooked, are kidney-shaped, creamy white in colour, and have a soft and fluffy texture and a delicately nutty flavour. These protein-packed beans can be added to soups, stews and salads. Here, they are combined with tuna, which is a good source of vitamin B12, a vitamin that assists in the formation of red blood cells and can help prevent the development of anaemia.

SERVES 2

1 tbsp olive oil
1 onion, finely chopped
1 tsp white wine vinegar
1 garlic clove, crushed, or 1 tsp garlic purée
400g tin cannellini beans, drained
185g tin tuna (in water), drained and flaked
Pinch of freshly ground black pepper

1   Heat half the oil in a frying pan over a medium heat, add the onion and fry for 5–7 minutes until soft and beginning to brown.
2   Put the remaining oil in a screw-top jar with the vinegar and garlic, seal with a lid and shake well.
3   Gently mix together the onion, beans and flaked tuna in a bowl. Drizzle with the dressing, season with the black pepper and serve.

Tuscan Bread Salad

This classic Italian bread salad is also called panzanella. Juicy tomatoes combined with the sweetness of basil makes this a good accompaniment to fish dishes and it works well with the Chicken Chasseur on page 158.

SERVES 4
¼ cucumber, washed and roughly chopped
1 red onion, thinly sliced or roughly chopped
2 very ripe tomatoes, washed and roughly chopped
½ small loaf country-style bread or a baguette, cut
   into large cubes
12 basil leaves, washed and roughly crushed

For the dressing
2 tbsp extra virgin olive oil
1 tbsp balsamic vinegar
½ tsp caster sugar
¼ tsp freshly ground black pepper

1 Place the cucumber, onion, tomatoes and bread in a bowl.
2 Whisk the dressing ingredients together in a small bowl and add the basil. Give it a good stir then add it to the salad. The bread should feel moist but not soggy. Serve immediately.

Greek Salad

Dressings make salads more appetising but bear in mind that only a little is required to bump up the flavour. This particular dressing includes fresh garlic which boosts the production of white blood cells in the body that fight off bacteria, fungus and viruses.

SERVES 2

For the salad

2 tomatoes, washed and cut into wedges
¼ cucumber, peeled and thinly sliced
120g feta or low-fat salad cheese, cubed
½ red onion, thinly sliced
6 pitted black olives, sliced
A few flat-leaf parsley leaves, washed and chopped

For the dressing

1 garlic clove, crushed, or 1 tsp garlic purée
1 tbsp balsamic vinegar
Pinch of sea salt (optional)
¼ tsp freshly ground black pepper
½ tsp dried oregano
1 tbsp extra virgin olive oil (preferably Greek)
1 tbsp lemon juice
1 tbsp runny honey

1   Combine the salad ingredients in a bowl.
2   Mix the dressing ingredients together in a screw-top jar. Pour the dressing over the salad just before serving.

Creole-style Green Salad

Hailing from Louisiana in the United States, Creole cuisine combines various styles of cooking with French, Spanish and West African influences.

A shallot is a type of small and elongated onion that has a mild and slightly sweet flavour, with a hint of garlic. It can be used raw in salads and dressings. If you are substituting shallots for onion, bear in mind that one small onion is the equivalent of three shallots. This recipe uses both red onion and shallot for added bite.

SERVES 2

For the dressing
1 medium shallot, finely diced
2 tbsp sherry vinegar (or your favourite vinegar)
2 tsp Dijon or Creole mustard (see box below)
3 or 4 drops of Tabasco hot sauce (optional)
2 tbsp extra virgin olive oil
¼ tsp freshly ground black pepper

For the salad
2 large handfuls of mixed green salad leaves, washed and chopped
8–10 croutons (optional)
1 red onion, very thinly sliced

1 For the dressing, put the shallot, vinegar, mustard and hot sauce, if using, in a mug. Gradually whisk in the oil until the dressing is emulsified, then add the pepper.
2 Plate the salad leaves in a bowl and sprinkle the croutons on top, if using. Place a small mound of the red onion in the centre. Drizzle over the dressing just before serving.

> To create your own Creole mustard, combine 6 tablespoons of Dijon mustard with ½ teaspoon of Worcestershire sauce, and a spicy element such as hot sauce or Tabasco sauce.

Potato Salad

Although potato is not classed as one of your five a day, the skin of potatoes contains fibre which aids digestion.

SERVES 2

250g baby potatoes, such as Charlotte, washed and
   thinly sliced
1 red onion, finely chopped
A few flat-leaf parsley leaves, washed and chopped
2 dill fronds, washed
1 tbsp capers, drained (optional)

For the Dijon vinaigrette
1 tbsp extra virgin olive oil
1 tbsp white wine vinegar
1 tsp Dijon mustard
¼ tsp freshly ground black pepper
Pinch of ground coriander

1   Place the sliced potatoes in a saucepan and cover with cold
    water. Bring to the boil and simmer until the potatoes are
    tender.
2   Meanwhile, put the vinaigrette ingredients in a small bowl
    and whisk until well combined.
3   When the potatoes are ready, remove from the heat and
    drain. Place the potatoes on a baking sheet or tray and
    immediately add the vinaigrette. Toss to coat. Let the
    potatoes sit for 10 minutes to allow the flavours to combine.
    Add the onion, fresh herbs, and capers, if using, and toss to
    combine. Transfer to a serving dish or bowl and serve at
    room temperature.

Coleslaw

Crème fraîche is a thick soured cream often used in French cooking. It is thicker and less tangy than soured cream and won't curdle when heated, however soured cream is less calorific.

SERVES 6

6 tbsp soured cream or crème fraîche
½ tsp Dijon mustard
2 tbsp mayonnaise
½ white cabbage or red cabbage, roughly chopped and washed
2 carrots, peeled and washed

1. Mix the soured cream or crème fraîche, mustard and mayonnaise together in a bowl.
2. Use a grater attachment on a food processor or a medium to fine box grater to grate the cabbage and carrots. Tip the vegetables into the bowl and stir through the dressing.
3. This salad will keep in a sealed container in the fridge for up to 3 days.

Olive Wreath Holiday Appetiser

This is a fun way to jazz up fresh ingredients, by creating a ring with some fresh herbs and filling the centre with salad ingredients, then serving as a sharing plate. The dressing adds flavour to the tomatoes and mozzarella.

SERVES 6

8 fresh rosemary branches, washed
20–30 mixed pitted olives
16 cherry tomatoes, washed
12 mini mozzarella balls
10 jalapeños, finely chopped (optional)

For the dressing
2 tbsp extra virgin olive oil
¼ tsp freshly ground black pepper
2 tbsp balsamic vinegar
1 tsp runny honey
Pinch of sea salt

1 Lay a ring of fresh rosemary around the edge of a plate, creating a 'wreath'.
2 Place the mixed olives, cherry tomatoes and mini mozzarella balls inside the ring of rosemary. Scatter the jalapeños over the salad ingredients, if using. Stack as much as you can within the ring while still maintaining a wreath shape.
3 Mix the dressing ingredients together and drizzle it over the 'wreath' just before serving.

Muhammara

Muhammara, a dip from Aleppo in Syria, is made from peppers, chilli peppers, breadcrumbs, olive oil and pomegranate molasses. The pomegranate molasses bring both tartness and sweetness to the dip. Muhammara is eaten as a dip with bread, as a spread for toast, and as a sauce for kebabs, grilled meats and fish.

SERVES 6-8

3 red peppers (drained peppers from a 460g jar can be used)
50g fresh breadcrumbs
½ tbsp lemon juice
1 tbsp pomegranate molasses
1½ tsp ground cumin
1 tsp chilli flakes
1 small garlic clove, crushed, or 1 tsp garlic purée
50g walnuts, finely chopped by hand
2 tbsp extra virgin olive oil, plus extra for drizzling

1   If you're using fresh peppers, preheat the oven to 200°C/400°F/Gas 6. Put the peppers on a baking tray and roast for 30–35 minutes, turning them occasionally, until they are cooked and the skin is blackened. Put the peppers in a bowl, cover with cling film and, once cool enough to handle, peel and discard the skin and seeds.

2   Pat the roasted peppers or peppers from a jar dry and place in a mortar. Add the breadcrumbs, lemon juice, pomegranate molasses, cumin, chilli flakes and garlic. Work the mixture with a pestle until well combined, but not so much that the peppers no longer have a noticeable texture. You can use the pulse setting on a food processor if you have one.

3   Stir through the walnuts and the olive oil. Spoon the dip into a shallow bowl, using the back of a spoon to give it a wavy texture, and drizzle with a little olive oil. Serve at room temperature.

Beetroot and Kidney Bean Salad

Beetroots contain vitamins and minerals such as potassium and vitamin C, but be mindful that the carbohydrates in beetroots are simple sugars such as glucose and fructose, so consume them in moderation.

Kidney beans are one of the best sources of plant proteins and they can help reduce blood sugar levels. If you're not used to a high-fibre diet, beware of over-consuming beans, which can cause digestive discomfort, gas and bloating.

SERVES 4

4 cooked beetroots (not in vinegar), cut into half-moons or semi circles

400g tin kidney beans, drained and rinsed (or 200g dried – see page 51 for cooking method)

4 spring onions, washed and cut into thin rounds

For the dressing
Juice of 1 lemon
2 tbsp extra virgin olive oil
1 tbsp pomegranate molasses
¼ tsp freshly ground black pepper
¼ tsp sea salt (optional)

1   Combine the dressing ingredients in a small bowl or ramekin and set aside.

2   Mix the beetroots and kidney beans together in a bowl. When ready to serve, combine the spring onions with the beetroots and kidney beans and pour over the dressing.

Tabbouleh

Tabbouleh, a traditional Levantine salad, is a popular accompaniment to many summer meals. Its main ingredient is parsley, which gives the salad a subtle and interesting flavour you don't get with most lettuce-based salads. This salad makes an ideal accompaniment to main meals (it's a delicious accompaniment to roast chicken), picnics and barbecues, or even a quick and healthy packed lunch. Although similar in texture to couscous (a type of pasta), bulgur wheat is a nutritious cereal grain made from parboiled cracked wheat.

SERVES 2

2 heaped tbsp bulgur wheat, rinsed

Handful of flat-leaf parsley leaves, washed and finely chopped

2 medium red tomatoes, washed and finely chopped

4 spring onions, washed and finely chopped

5–6 mint leaves, washed and finely chopped

2 tbsp lemon juice

2 tbsp extra virgin olive oil

1   Put the bulgur wheat in a small heatproof bowl and pour over enough boiling water to cover. Cover the bowl with cling film and allow to stand for 15 minutes until the grains are tender.

2   Place the bulgur wheat in a sieve and squeeze out any excess water with a spoon.

3   Mix all the vegetable ingredients and herbs in a serving bowl.

4   Five minutes before serving, add the lemon juice, olive oil and the bulgur wheat and mix together. Serve immediately.

Niçoise Pasta Salad

Young, tender green beans are a good source of vitamin C, dietary fibre, folate and vitamin K, which the body needs for blood clotting and helping wounds to heal. Green beans can retain their antioxidant qualities after brief cooking.

SERVES 2

100g penne pasta (ideally wholehwheat/wholemeal)
50g green beans, trimmed and halved
30g tin anchovy fillets in oil (about 4 anchovy fillets),
    drained and chopped
1 tbsp extra virgin olive oil
1 garlic clove, finely chopped
10 cherry tomatoes, washed and halved
6 black pitted olives
160g tin tuna (in water), drained
Juice of ½ lemon
Handful of basil leaves, washed and roughly chopped

1   Bring a large pan of water to the boil, add the penne, bring back to the boil and cook for about 10 minutes. Add the beans to the pan of pasta 5 minutes before the end of the cooking time.
2   Wipe the anchovies with kitchen paper to remove excess salt and oil.
3   While the pasta's cooking, heat the olive oil in a frying pan over a medium heat, add the garlic and anchovies, and fry gently for a couple of minutes, stirring to dissolve the anchovies in the oil. Add the halved tomatoes and cook for a few minutes more until just softened but not mushy.
4   Drain the pasta and beans and run under a cold tap to prevent the pasta from sticking. Return the pasta and beans to the same pan they were cooked in, then add the tomato mixture and olives. Flake in the tuna and add the lemon juice and basil. Heat through gently and serve.

Sides, dips and dunks

This section contains a selection of dishes that could complement meals from the lunch and evening meal chapters. There's no better way to know exactly what's going into the food you're eating than by making it yourself, and serving your meal with a side dish made from scratch can mean more vitamins, minerals, nutrients and fibre, with fewer empty calories than you may find in shop-bought processed food products. In addition, some of the sides in this section, such as the Pinto beans with Garlic and Allspice (page 109) and Tunisian-style Aubergines (page 112), could replace a main meal.

Cream Cheese and Cucumber on Rye

Rye bread is generally made with a combination of rye flour and rye grains. It's darker in colour and has a stronger and earthier taste than regular white or wholemeal bread. Rye bread has been linked to several potential health benefits such as improved heart and digestive health.

SERVES 2

4 tbsp cream cheese

1 tbsp blue cheese dressing

2 slices of rye bread

¼ cucumber, washed and cut into 5mm-thick rounds

5 or 6 black or green olives, pitted and finely chopped

1   In a small bowl, combine the cream cheese and blue cheese dressing. Spread the cheese mixture on the rye bread slices. Top with the cucumber rounds and olives.

2   Serve immediately.

Mashed Potatoes in a Microwave

Potatoes are naturally gluten-free, which make them a compatible choice for people suffering from coeliac disease or those who are gluten sensitive. Boiling, baking and steaming potatoes is better than frying them (which inevitably increases their calorie content). Potatoes should be eaten in moderation as part of a balanced diet.

SERVES 2
2 floury potatoes, peeled and cut into small chunks
180ml semi-skimmed milk
1 tbsp unsalted butter
¼ tsp freshly ground black pepper

1   Rinse the peeled potato chunks and put them in a large, microwave-safe dish or bowl. Cover the dish or bowl with cling film and cut a small slit in the top for steam to escape. Microwave on high for 8–11 minutes, or until the potatoes are tender. Using oven gloves, carefully remove the bowl from the microwave.
2   Heat the milk and the butter in the microwave until the butter has nearly melted.
3   Mash the potatoes with the milk and the butter using a fork. Season with the black pepper and serve.

Brussels Sprouts and Bacon

Brussels sprouts contain high levels of antioxidants, which are natural substances that may help prevent or delay some types of cell damage caused by free radicals. Free radicals are unstable molecules that the body produces as a reaction to environmental pressures.

SERVES 4

250g Brussels sprouts

1 tbsp extra virgin olive oil

70g smoked bacon lardons, or bacon or turkey rashers, cut into small pieces

4 tbsp double cream or crème fraîche

1 garlic clove, crushed, or 1 tsp garlic purée

¼ tsp freshly ground black pepper

1 Cut off and discard the bottom end of each sprout, along with any wilted or discoloured leaves, then slice them vertically to halve them and wash thoroughly.

2 Cook the sprouts in a saucepan of boiling water for about 5 minutes until slightly soft or al dente (firm to the bite). Drain, run under a cold tap until cold, then drain again and set aside.

3 Heat the oil in a frying pan over a medium heat, add the bacon pieces and sauté for 5–6 minutes. Remove from the pan and set aside. Add the cream and garlic to the pan and, when it comes to the boil, stir in the cooked sprouts. Sprinkle with the bacon and black pepper and serve.

Pinto Beans with Garlic and Allspice

This deliciously spiced piquant dish is a level up from baked beans and can be served as a main meal.

Although they were discovered thousands of miles apart, allspice and cloves are often confused because they contain the same compound, eugenol, which is a powerful antioxidant. Allspice is a bit more peppery than cloves, but has a hint of orange peel and a sweet flavour which works in savoury as well as sweet dishes.

Serve this bean dish with toasted wholemeal pitta breads.

SERVES 2

2 tbsp extra virgin olive oil

2 bay leaves

1 onion, finely chopped

2–3 garlic cloves, finely chopped

1 tsp tomato purée

½ tsp ground allspice

¼ tsp chilli flakes

400g tin pinto beans, drained and rinsed

500ml vegetable stock (can be made from a low-sodium or low-salt stock cube, or see recipe on page 74)

1   Heat the oil in a saucepan over a medium heat, add the bay leaves and stir, then tip in the onion and fry for 3–4 minutes until softened. Add the garlic and cook for a further 2–3 minutes until the garlic is soft, then mix in the tomato purée, allspice and chilli flakes and cook for 2 minutes, stirring occasionally. Tip in the pinto beans and sauté for a minute, then pour in the stock and simmer for 10–15 minutes until the beans are tender. Serve.

Green Beans with Lemon and Pepper Dressing

Without a doubt, lemon is the most useful of all fruits. It is packed with vitamin C, which helps boost the immune system.

Dressing vegetables while they're still warm helps them absorb some of the dressing, which means less dressing is needed. The very simple lemon and pepper dressing used to accompany these beans can be used for all kinds of veggies. Use this recipe to learn how to balance the oil and acidity in a simple dressing.

SERVES 4

1 unwaxed lemon
1 tbsp extra virgin olive oil
¼ tsp sea salt (optional)
Pinch of freshly ground black pepper
300g green beans, trimmed and washed

1 Grate the zest of the lemon into a large bowl using a fine grater. Cut the lemon in half and squeeze in the juice from one half. Add the olive oil and season with the sea salt, if using, and freshly ground black pepper to taste. Mix well.

2 Bring a saucepan of water to the boil, add the beans and cook for 4–5 minutes until tender but still bright green. Drain well, then tip the cooked beans into the bowl of dressing and toss everything together, making sure all the beans get coated. Have a taste and squeeze over the remaining lemon juice if you think it needs it, then serve.

3 The beans can be served hot, warm or at room temperature, but if they sit in the dressing too long, they will start to discolour, so either eat them straightaway or dress them just before you want to eat them.

Harissa Couscous

Couscous is made from durum wheat or semolina flour. The selenium in couscous can give your immune system a boost and is very easy to prepare, making it a healthier alternative to pasta.

This dish is a great accompaniment to the Tunisian-style Aubergines on page 112.

SERVES 2

120g couscous

90ml hot vegetable stock (can be made from a low-sodium or low-salt stock cube, or see recipe on page 74)

2 tsp harissa paste

1 tsp extra virgin olive oil

1 tsp lemon juice

6–8 cherry tomatoes, washed and halved

½ red onion, finely chopped

A few washed and chopped mint leaves

1   Tip the couscous into a heatproof bowl, pour over the stock, cover and set aside for 10 minutes.

2   Fluff up the couscous with a fork, then mix in the harissa paste. Add the olive oil and lemon juice and stir thoroughly, then add the tomatoes and mix again. Scatter with the onion and mint.

3   The couscous will keep in the fridge (without the mint), covered, for up to 4 days.

Tunisian-style Aubergines

Packed with dietary fibre and rich in antioxidants, aubergines have the potential to lower cholesterol and help you manage your weight. They're a versatile vegetable that can be used in salads, stews and dips. Fresh herbs such as coriander and mint feature heavily in Tunisian cuisine. This is a great dish to serve with either wholemeal pitta breads or couscous.

SERVES 4

700g aubergines, washed and cut into 1cm cubes
3 tbsp extra virgin olive oil
1 onion, finely chopped
4 garlic cloves, finely chopped
1 green chilli, finely chopped
1 tbsp tomato purée
1 tsp ground cumin
¼ tsp sea salt (optional)
¼ tsp freshly ground black pepper

To serve
2 tbsp washed and finely chopped fresh mint
2 tbsp washed and finely chopped coriander leaves
4 tbsp Greek-style low-fat yogurt

1 Preheat the oven to 180°C/350°F/Gas 4 and line a baking tray with greaseproof paper.
2 Spread the cubed aubergine out on the lined baking tray, drizzle over 1 tablespoon of the oil, and roast in the oven for 20 minutes.

3 Meanwhile, heat the remaining 2 tablespoons of oil in a large frying pan over a medium-high heat, add the onion and fry for 5–6 minutes until softened and lightly golden, then add the garlic and fry for another minute. Tip in the green chilli and fry for a further minute, then add the tomato purée, cumin and salt, if using. Stir well.

4 Tip in the roasted aubergine and black pepper and cook for 3–4 minutes until the aubergines have absorbed the flavours of the spices.

5 Remove from the heat, scatter with the mint and coriander and serve hot with a tablespoon of the yogurt for each serving.

Spiced and Herby Carrots

Star anise is a spice that not only imparts a liquorice-like flavour and a delightful fragrance to food, but is also rich in antioxidants and aids digestion. It is used predominantly in Chinese dishes and beautifully complements the sweetness of carrots to create something more than just boiled vegetables.

SERVES 2-3

4–6 carrots, peeled, washed and thickly sliced
½ tsp dried thyme
1 garlic clove, crushed, or 1 tsp garlic purée
1 star anise
1 bay leaf
1 tsp extra virgin olive oil
½ tsp cumin seeds
1 tbsp unsalted butter

1   Put the carrots, thyme, garlic, star anise and bay leaf in a saucepan and just cover with water. Bring to the boil, then reduce the heat and simmer for 10–15 minutes until soft and tender. Remove from the heat and allow to cool. Once cooled, remove the carrots from the water with a slotted spoon.

2   Heat the olive oil in a large frying pan over a medium heat, add the cumin seeds and let them sizzle, then tip in the carrots and fry for about 5 minutes until golden brown all over. Reduce the heat, add the butter, and roll the carrots around until they are lovely and glossy, then remove from the heat and serve.

Egg and Anchovy Crispbread

Anchovies are high in omega 3 fatty acids which are known to have anti-inflammatory properties and can help lower cholesterol. Bear in mind, though, that tinned anchovies contain a lot of salt. The white and yolk of eggs are rich in nutrients.

SERVES 4

6 hard-boiled free-range eggs, shelled and finely chopped

2 tbsp finely chopped red onion

2 tbsp washed and finely snipped chives

Handful of dill, washed and finely chopped, plus extra fronds, to serve

6 anchovy fillets in oil, drained, patted dry with kitchen paper and chopped

¼ tsp ground white pepper

4 slices of crispbread

Lemon halves, to serve

1 Combine the eggs, onion, chives, dill, anchovies and ground white pepper. Spread on crispbread, scatter with extra dill and serve with lemon halves, for squeezing.

Party Potato Skins

This is a once-in-a-while treat, because potatoes are rich in carbohydrates which can affect your blood sugar levels. Most of a potato's fibre, which assists in digestion, is found in its skin.

Serve with a crisp green salad.

SERVES 2

2 baking potatoes, scrubbed, washed and pierced all over
   with a fork
1 tbsp extra virgin olive oil
50g Cheddar cheese, grated
2 spring onions, washed and finely chopped
1 tsp Dijon mustard
1 tsp butter

1   Preheat the oven to 180°C/350°F/Gas 4.
2   Cook the potatoes in a saucepan of boiling water for about 10
    minutes, then carefully remove them from the saucepan and
    place them on a baking tray. Drizzle with the olive oil, then
    rub the oil into the potatoes. Bake in the oven for 30 minutes,
    or until the potatoes are tender.
3   Remove from the oven and carefully cut the potatoes in half,
    scoop out the middle of the potatoes (being careful not to
    split the skins) and transfer the potato flesh to a mixing
    bowl. Add the grated cheese, spring onions, mustard and
    butter to the potato filling and combine.
4   Scoop the filling into the potato skin vessels and bake in the
    oven on the baking tray for 10–15 minutes, or until golden
    brown on top.

Garlic Butter Toast

This is a nice way to get that takeaway fix when you fancy preparing a pasta dish or a hearty soup (try it with the Pizza Soup on page 82).

You can keep the garlic butter in the fridge to use at a later time. You could also add extra fresh washed and chopped herbs such as thyme and tarragon to the butter before spreading.

SERVES 4

4 tsp unsalted butter
2 garlic cloves, crushed, or 2 tsp garlic purée
4 slices of wholemeal bread, each cut diagonally in half
A few washed and chopped parsley leaves

1   Preheat the oven to 180°C/350°F/Gas 4.
2   Melt the butter in the microwave (it will only take a few seconds) and mix in the garlic.
3   Spread the garlic butter on one side of each slice of bread. Place the bread slices butter side up on a baking sheet and cook for 1–2 minutes until the toast is lightly browned.
4   Remove from the oven and garnish with the parsley.

Mackerel Pâté

Tinned mackerel is full of omega 3 fatty acids, which are essential for keeping the heart healthy and aiding brain function. In traditional folk medicine, tarragon has been used in small amounts to treat pain for conditions such as osteoarthritis.

This versatile recipe works just as well as a sandwich filling, with wholemeal bread and slices of cucumber, as it does spread thickly on toast, oatcakes or crackers.

SERVES 2

120–125g tin mackerel fillets in oil, or similar tinned
   oily fish fillets, drained
1 tsp Dijon mustard or ½ tsp English mustard
1 tbsp crème fraîche or cream cheese
Pinch of cayenne pepper or chilli powder
Pinch of freshly ground black pepper
1 tsp lemon juice
A few leaves of fresh tarragon (optional)

1 Tip the drained fish into the bowl of a food processor and add the mustard, crème fraîche or cream cheese, cayenne or chilli powder, black pepper and lemon juice. Blitz to a thick paste, stopping several times as you go to scrape the mixture down from the sides of the processor. Taste and add more pepper or lemon juice, if necessary.
2 Garnish with the tarragon, if using.

Thyme, Sage and Onion Stuffing

Sage may help lower blood sugar levels, and hazelnuts are rich in vitamin E, which evidence has suggested could help offer protection against cell damage. However, if you're prone to cold sores, do omit the hazelnuts from the recipe. This stuffing is perfect for a Sunday roast dinner.

SERVES 4

2 onions, finely chopped
2 slices of wholemeal bread (stale bread is fine)
20g hazelnuts, finely chopped
30g dried apricots, finely chopped, or 1 washed apple
Handful of sage leaves, washed and chopped
Handful of thyme leaves
½ tsp freshly ground black pepper
¼ tsp sea salt (optional)
1 small egg, beaten
1 tbsp softened butter or extra virgin olive oil

1 Preheat the oven to 180°C/350°F/Gas 4.
2 Put the chopped onions in a microwave-safe bowl and cover with cling film. Pierce the film a few times to create vents for the steam, then microwave for 3 minutes until softened, then remove from the microwave, stir, replace the cling film and microwave for another 3 minutes.
3 Using a blender or food processor, blitz the bread and the hazelnuts until the mixture has the consistency of breadcrumbs. Transfer to a bowl.
4 Put the microwaved onions in the blender and blend to a paste, then add them to the bowl of bread and hazelnuts. If using an apple, grate it into the bowl and throw away the core (or add the apricots), then add the sage, thyme, pepper and salt, if using. Add the egg with the butter or olive oil and combine with a spoon until the mixture comes together and forms a thick paste. Press into a shallow non-stick baking dish to a thickness of about 2.5cm and bake on the top shelf of the oven for 20 minutes, until golden.

Tartare Sauce

Have a go at making your own tartare sauce with this easy recipe. Shallots and onions are high in antioxidants and may help improve blood sugar levels.

This is perfect paired with the Pesto-crusted Cod Fillet (page 64) or the Party Potato Skins (page 116).

SERVES 4

4 tbsp mayonnaise
1 gherkin, drained and finely chopped
1 tsp capers, drained (optional)
1 small shallot or onion, finely chopped
1 tsp lemon juice
2 tbsp washed and finely chopped flat-leaf parsley leaves
¼ tsp freshly ground black pepper

1   Place all the ingredients in a bowl and mix. Cover and chill in the fridge.
2   Remove from the fridge 5 minutes before serving. This can be stored, covered, in the fridge for up to 2–3 days.

Apple Sauce

The soluble fibre in apples can aid digestion and help lower cholesterol. They're a good source of vitamin C, too. This apple sauce can be used as an accompaniment to lean roast chicken breast, Cream Cheese and Cucumber on Rye (page 106), or Brussels Sprouts and Bacon (page 108).

MAKES ABOUT 250G

2 Bramley apples, washed
1 tsp lemon juice
2 tsp caster sugar

1 Using a sharp vegetable peeler or a paring knife, remove the apple peel. Quarter the apple, cut out the central core and discard.
2 Put the apples in a saucepan with the lemon juice, sugar and 120ml water. Bring to the boil, then reduce the heat and simmer for 10–15 minutes, stirring, until the apples are tender and cooked through. Mash the apples to make a smoother sauce.
3 Serve, or leave to cool and store in the fridge for up to 7–10 days.

Boston Beans

Molasses is the dark and syrupy sweet by-product that is produced during the extraction of sugars from sugar cane and sugar beets. Predominantly used in the Caribbean and America for making bean and barbecue dishes, it has a more intense and richer flavour than sugar, and should be used in moderation.

Serve with a jacket potato and the Iceberg Salad on page 86.

SERVES 2

1 tbsp extra virgin olive oil
1 bay leaf
1 onion, finely chopped
2 rashers of smoked bacon, or chicken sausages or turkey rashers, cut into 2cm pieces
1 tsp dark brown sugar or molasses
¼ tsp freshly ground black pepper
¼ tsp Dijon or English mustard powder
1 tbsp Worcestershire sauce
415g tin baked beans

1   Heat the oil in a saucepan over a medium heat, add the bay leaf and sauté for a few seconds, then add the onion and cook for a further 5–6 minutes until softened. Add the bacon, sausages or rashers and cook for another 3–4 minutes, then add the sugar or molasses, pepper, mustard and Worcestershire sauce. Cook for a couple of minutes until well combined, then tip in the beans and cook for 5 minutes more.
2   Remove from the heat and serve.

Shawarma Sauce

Shawarma is a Middle Eastern dish of meat cut into thin slices, accompanied with salads and sauces such as this tahini-based creamy recipe.

Serve with a salad, or the Tabbouleh on page 103.

SERVES 2

50g tahini (sesame paste)
1 garlic clove, crushed or minced, or 1 tsp garlic purée
2 tsp lemon juice
2 tbsp unsweetened natural yogurt
¼ tsp ground cumin
1 tbsp washed and finely chopped flat-leaf parsley leaves
A sprinkling of hot smoked paprika

1   Put the tahini and garlic in a bowl, then whisk in the lemon juice and yogurt to form a creamy sauce. Stir in the cumin and parsley, sprinkle with the paprika and serve.

Chinese-style Crispy Kale Seaweed

Kale, a cruciferous vegetable that belongs to the cabbage family, is one of the most nutrient-dense and fibre-rich foods available, and it can boost digestive health. This can be served with Chinese-style Fried Rice on page 66.

SERVES 4

A few handfuls of kale, washed
A little drizzle of extra virgin olive oil or sunflower oil
Pinch of sea salt
Pinch of granulated sugar

1 Preheat the oven to 220°C/420°F/Gas 7.
2 Pull the kale leaves from their stalks: hold the end of the stalk with one hand and slide your other hand tightly down towards the leaves, pulling them from the stalk as you go. Finely chop the leaves.
3 Drizzle the oil over the leaves in a bowl and toss to coat, then add the salt and sugar. Arrange the leaves spread out in a single layer on an ovenproof baking tray or dish. Bake for about 5 minutes, until deep green and crispy. Check after 2–3 minutes to make sure they're not burnt.

Indian Salad Dressing

Most Indian salads are dressed with a little chilli, lemon juice and salt – adding spices (and herbs too) is a great way to embellish and add extra flavour to ordinary salads. It works particularly well with salads made with chopped tomatoes and sliced red onions.

SERVES 4

3 tbsp light olive oil
2 tsp peeled and grated root ginger or ginger paste
2 garlic cloves, crushed, or 2 tsp garlic purée
1 green chilli, finely chopped
½ tsp ground cumin
½ tsp ground coriander
¼ tsp freshly ground black pepper
4 tbsp washed and roughly chopped coriander leaves
1 tsp runny honey
2 tsp lemon juice
¼ tsp sea salt (optional)

1 Heat 1 tablespoon of the oil in a small saucepan over a medium heat, add the ginger and garlic and cook for 3–4 minutes, being careful that they don't burn. Remove from the heat and transfer to a blender or a mortar. Add the remaining oil, green chilli, cumin, ground coriander, black pepper, coriander leaves, honey, lemon juice and salt, if using. Blend or pound with a pestle until smooth then chill in the fridge until needed – it will keep for up to a week.

2 When ready to use, mix into a salad and serve.

Hummus

No hummus tastes as good as the one you make at home. Besides, you know what ingredients you have put in it and it involves no cooking.

SERVES 4-6
400g tin chickpeas
1 garlic clove, crushed, or 1 tsp garlic purée
1 tbsp tahini
2 tbsp extra virgin olive oil
Juice of ½ lemon
¼ tsp ground cumin
¼ tsp mild chilli powder
Pinch of sea salt (optional)

To garnish
Pinch of sweet smoked paprika
Pitted black olives

1 Drain the chickpeas and reserve the liquid.
2 Blend the chickpeas with the garlic, tahini, olive oil, lemon juice, 1–2 tablepoons of the chickpea liquid, the ground cumin and chilli powder and salt, if using, in a food processor. The hummus should have a soft dropping consistency that's not too runny.
3 Serve the hummus in a bowl, garnished with a sprinkling of paprika and black olives.

Use freshly ground cumin if you like: toasting ½ teaspoon of seeds lightly for 30 seconds in a dry pan over a medium heat before grinding them in a spice mill or a pestle and mortar to a medium-fine powder will help to bring out their aroma.

Brown Basmati Rice with Garlic

Brown basmati rice has more fibre than white basmati rice and a lower glycemic index, meaning that it is a better option for those watching their blood glucose levels. However, if your digestive system is more sensitive, use white rice instead (though bear in mind that the cooking time for white rice is considerably shorter).

Try serving this with Tarka Dal on page 148.

SERVES 3-4

200g brown basmati rice, washed
1 tbsp extra virgin olive oil or sunflower oil
3–4 garlic cloves, finely chopped
Juice of ½ lemon
a few sprigs of curly-leaf parsley, washed and chopped
    (optional)

1   Put the rice in a medium saucepan (that has a tight-fitting lid), add 625ml of just-boiled water and bring to the boil. Stir once, cover and reduce the heat to low. Simmer for 45–50 minutes (do not lift the lid or stir). Remove from the heat and let it stand, covered, for 5 minutes, then remove the lid and fluff the rice with a fork.

2   Heat the oil in a large frying pan or saucepan over a medium heat, add the garlic and sauté for a couple of minutes until it begins to lightly brown (be careful not to burn the garlic or it will be bitter). Add the cooked rice and sauté for 1–2 minutes, then mix in the lemon juice. Fluff with a fork, sprinkle with the parsley, if using, and serve hot.

Parsley Rice

Rich in vitamins, parsley is a good source of vitamins A and C and comes from the same botanical family as coriander. However, their flavour notes are different, with parsley being milder yet peppery in taste. It's a great all-rounder and gives a zesty kick to this recipe.

SERVES 4

1 tbsp extra virgin olive oil

200g long-grain white rice, washed

500ml vegetable stock (can be made from a low-sodium or low-salt stock cube, or see recipe on page 74)

2 tbsp washed and finely chopped curly-leaf parsley

1   Heat the oil in a saucepan over a medium heat, add the rice and sauté for a minute, then add the stock and bring to the boil. Reduce the heat, cover and cook for 12–15 minutes until the rice grains are tender. Remove from the heat and use a fork to fluff up the rice before sprinkling in the parsley.

Salsa

Salsa, a condiment served in Mexican cuisine, is predominantly made from tomatoes and chillies. This salsa works well as an accompaniment for Pinto Beans with Garlic and Allspice (page 109) and Brown Basmati Rice with Garlic (page 127).

SERVES 4
1 tbsp extra virgin olive oil
Juice of ½ lime
½ tsp ground cumin
Generous pinch of chilli flakes
4 medium tomatoes, washed and finely chopped
1 red onion, finely chopped

1   Mix the oil, lime juice, ground cumin and chilli flakes in a bowl. Just before serving, mix in the tomatoes and red onion. To make the salsa smoother, blend the ingredients in a blender or food processor.
2   The salsa will keep in the fridge for up to 2 days.

Minted Yogurt Dip

Mint plays an important role in aiding digestion, as the aroma of the herb activates the salivary glands to secrete the relevant enzymes that deal with the process of digestion. This Indian-style yogurt dip (also known as raita) works well with biryani rice dishes, Turmeric and Mushroom Rice (page 69) and Brown Basmati Rice with Garlic (page 127). It can be made a day in advance.

SERVES 4

½ tsp cumin seeds or ground cumin
50g mint leaves, hard stalks removed and leaves washed
30g coriander leaves, washed and roughly chopped
1 green chilli, roughly chopped
¼ tsp caster sugar
Pinch of sea salt
Pinch of freshly ground black pepper
100g unsweetened natural yogurt, whisked

1   If you are using cumin seeds, heat a dry frying pan over a medium heat, add the cumin seeds and toast for about 30 seconds until you can smell the aroma of the seeds. Remove from the heat and set aside. When cooled, grind to a medium-fine powder in a spice mill or a pestle and mortar.

2   Put the mint and coriander leaves in a blender with the green chilli, sugar, salt and black pepper and grind to a thick paste. To help bring everything together, add a tablespoon of the yogurt into the blender.

3   Place the green mixture in a bowl and mix in the remaining yogurt. Sprinkle over the ground cumin and serve chilled.

Guacamole

Often regarded as a superfood, avocados are high in potassium which supports healthy blood pressure levels. Chunky or smooth, the simple recipe requires just a few basic ingredients. Guacamole translates as 'avocado sauce', and it's perfect spooned on top of a salad or served with tortilla chips. It can be made up to a day in advance.

SERVES 2
2 ripe avocados, stoned and roughly chopped
2 tomatoes, washed and finely chopped
Juice of 1 lime
1 garlic clove, crushed, or 1 tsp garlic purée
A few washed and finely chopped coriander leaves
¼ tsp freshly ground black pepper

1   Put the avocados in a bowl and briefly mash with a fork, leaving some chunky pieces for texture. Gently mix in the tomatoes, lime juice, garlic and coriander leaves. Season with the pepper and serve.

Baharat Spice Blend

Making your own spice blends ensures that you know what's in them – many shop-bought blends could contain salt and sugar. This Middle Eastern spice mix adds depth and flavour to sauces, soups, grains and vegetables. I've included turmeric for extra pizzazz and because it boosts the spice blend's anti-inflammatory properties.

MAKES 30G

2 tsp coriander seeds
1 tbsp cumin seeds
½ tsp whole cloves
2 tsp black peppercorns
½ cinnamon stick (about 2cm)
Seeds of 4–6 green cardamom pods
1 heaped tsp ground turmeric
A good grating of nutmeg
2 tbsp paprika (not the smoked variety)

1 Put the whole spices in a small dry frying pan and heat over a low-medium heat for 2–3 minutes until you can smell the aroma of the spices (make sure they do not burn). Remove from the heat and allow to cool, then put the spices in a spice mill or a mortar and grind to a medium-fine powder. Add the remaining ground and grated spices and mix well.

2 Store the blend in an airtight container, preferably away from sunlight, heat and moisture, and use when required. It will keep well for up to 3 months.

Dinner

You should aim to eat dinner approximately four to five hours after eating lunch. After 5–6pm, your body's metabolic rate starts to slow down. Keep in mind that the longer you give your body between your last meal and your bedtime, the better your body performs a lot of maintenance tasks overnight, such as resting and renewing. If it's still busy digesting, those other tasks don't get taken care of, and eating too close to your bedtime can increase the risk of heartburn and indigestion and leaves the body in a high-alert state, which interferes with the circadian rhythm and makes it harder to fall asleep. It's important to go to bed feeling light, not full; this way you sleep better and wake up energised and hungry for a big breakfast.

It's best to eat lean meals in the evening. Eating hearty meals in the daytime instead of the evening can lead to weight loss and better health in general.

The dishes in this chapter are light and easy to digest, with lean chicken meals and indulgent vegetable suggestions.

Saag Paneer – Spinach and Indian Cheese

Paneer, a type of Indian cheese made from cow's or buffalo's milk, is rich in calcium and a healthy addition to your diet if eaten in moderation. Vitamin-rich spinach contains nutrients responsible for improving eyesight and boosting the immune system. Try not to overcook spinach, as this impacts its folate content.

Serve with toasted wholemeal pitta breads.

SERVES 4

3 tbsp sunflower or rapeseed oil
1 tsp cumin seeds
1 onion, finely chopped
2 garlic cloves, chopped
2 green chillies, finely chopped
500g spinach leaves, thoroughly washed
½ tsp ground coriander
¼ tsp sea salt (optional)
1 tsp lemon juice
50g paneer, cut into 2.5cm cubes
½ tsp garam masala
1 tsp peeled and grated root ginger or ginger paste

1   Heat 2 tablespoons of the oil in a large non-stick saucepan over a medium heat, add the cumin seeds, and when they begin to sizzle, tip in the onion. Fry for 5–7 minutes until softened and lightly browned, then add the garlic and chillies and continue to fry for 5–7 minutes. Mix in the spinach leaves and cook for 5 minutes until they have wilted, then add the ground coriander and salt, if using. Cook for another 30 seconds. Place the mixture in a food processor or blender and blend until almost a smooth paste. Sprinkle in the lemon juice.

2   Heat the remaining tablespoon of oil in the same non-stick pan over a medium heat, then tip in the paneer cubes, stir and cook for a few minutes. Return the blended spinach to the pan and mix well. Add the garam masala and ginger and mix, then cook for another minute. Serve.

Med Veg Medley

This dish doesn't take too long to knock up and quorn adds a meaty texture to the medley.

Quorn is a mycoprotein made from a fungus that's found in the soil and then fermented in huge vats. If you are opting for quorn as a source of meat replacement protein, choose the simplest type of quorn you can find, that has been through the least processing during manufacture and has the fewest added ingredients.

Serve hot with couscous.

SERVES 4

1 tbsp extra virgin olive oil

300g quorn pieces (roughly 2cm pieces)

1 onion, finely chopped

1 carrot, peeled, washed and cut into thick discs

2 garlic cloves, thickly sliced

200g tinned chopped tomatoes

250ml chicken stock (can be made from a low-sodium or low-salt stock cube)

1 tsp dried mixed herbs

¼ tsp freshly ground black pepper

1 yellow pepper, deseeded and cut into thin strips

1 Heat the oil in a large saucepan over a medium heat, then add the quorn and fry for 3–4 minutes or until nicely golden brown all over. Remove from the pan and set to one side.
2 Add the onion and carrot to the saucepan and fry, stirring, for 6–7 minutes, or until the onion is soft and translucent. Add the garlic and cook for 2 more minutes, then return the quorn pieces to the pan along with any juices. Pour in the tomatoes and stock, add the mixed herbs and mix well to make sure everything is well combined.
3 Season with the pepper, cover, and simmer gently for 20 minutes until the sauce is thickened slightly. Add the yellow pepper and cook for a further 2 minutes, then remove from the heat and serve.

Mexican-style Quorn or Lamb Tacos

Tortillas are round Mexican flatbreads made from cornmeal or sometimes wheat flour. A taco is a filled tortilla.

SERVES 4

1 tbsp extra virgin olive oil or sunflower oil

1 onion, finely chopped

4 garlic cloves, finely chopped

1 tsp ground cumin

1/4 tsp sweet smoked paprika

Pinch of chilli flakes

1 1/2 tbsp dried oregano

2 tsp chipotle paste

500g quorn pieces, minced lamb or minced quorn

400g tin chopped tomatoes

4 tortillas

To serve

2 baby gem or 1 small iceberg lettuce, washed and finely shredded

1 small red onion, thinly sliced

A few washed and chopped coriander leaves

40g Cheddar cheese, grated

6 tbsp natural Greek-style yogurt

1. Heat the oil in a saucepan over a medium heat, add the onion and garlic and cook for 5–7 minutes or until softened and golden. Tip in the cumin, paprika and chilli flakes and stir for a minute, then add the oregano. Stir in the chipotle paste and cook for 1 minute, then add the mince or pieces of quorn and cook until it turns brown. Mix in the tomatoes and cook for another 4–5 minutes until the sauce thickens.

2. Heat the tortillas in a dry frying pan over a low heat for a minute on each side, or 30 seconds in a microwave.

3. To make the tacos, spoon some of the filling onto the warmed tortillas, scatter with the lettuce, red onion, coriander leaves and grated cheese. Top with yogurt and serve.

Tibetan Thukpa Stew with Chicken

This is a Northeast Indian version of a chicken stew which generally includes wheat noodles – leaving these out, as I've done here, makes the depth of flavours more intense.

Bok choy, pak choi or Chinese white cabbage belongs to the cruciferous family of vegetables. These vegetables are a good source of nutrients with powerful antioxidant properties that help protect cells against damage and are low in calories.

SERVES 4

500g boneless and skinless chicken breasts, each cut in half

2cm piece of cinnamon stick

2 bay leaves

1 star anise

2 tbsp sunflower or rapeseed oil

1 onion, finely chopped

1 tsp peeled and grated root ginger or ginger paste

4 garlic cloves, finely chopped

2 celery sticks, washed and roughly chopped

2 carrots, peeled, washed and thinly sliced

2 heads washed and roughly chopped pak choi or bok choy leaves

1 tsp fennel seeds

2 cloves

1 green chilli, finely chopped

1 tbsp low-sodium (low-salt) soy sauce

1 tsp malt vinegar

½ tsp ground white pepper

1 tsp lime juice

A few coriander leaves, washed and chopped, to serve

1   Fill a saucepan with 500ml water, immerse the chicken pieces with the cinnamon, bay leaves and star anise, and place over a medium heat. Bring to the boil then reduce the heat and simmer for 20 minutes. Once the chicken pieces are cooked through, remove the chicken pieces and set aside. Strain the stock through a sieve into a heatproof bowl or jug and set aside.

2   Heat the oil in another saucepan over a medium heat, add the onion, ginger, garlic, celery and carrots and sauté for 3–4 minutes, then add the cooked chicken to the vegetables and mix well. Add the pak choi or bok choy leaves, fennel seeds and cloves and sauté for a minute or two until you can smell the aroma of these spices. Pour in the reserved stock, mix in the chilli, cover and simmer for 5 minutes.

3   Season with the soy sauce, malt vinegar, pepper and lime juice. Stir well, then remove the chicken pieces from the broth, chop into smaller pieces and immerse them again in the broth. Garnish with the coriander leaves and serve hot.

Chicken Shawarma

Shawarma is a Middle Eastern dish comprising of thinly sliced meat or chicken served with vegetables and a tahini-based dip. Tahini, a paste made from toasted and ground sesame seeds, imparts a light, nutty flavour to foods. It's best known as a key ingredient in hummus. Tahini is full of healthy fats, vitamins and minerals, and is a great source of phosphorus and manganese, both of which play vital roles in bone health. Sesame seeds may decrease risk factors for heart disease and the risk of developing Type 2 diabetes.

SERVES 2

120g unsweetened natural yogurt
1 tbsp extra virgin olive oil
2 tbsp malt vinegar
2 garlic cloves, crushed, or 2 tsp garlic puree
1 tsp ground white pepper
½ tsp ground mixed spice or allspice
1½ tbsp lemon juice or juice of ½ lemon
250g skinless and boneless chicken thighs or breasts, thinly sliced
2 wholemeal pitta breads

For the tahini sauce
2–3 garlic cloves, crushed, or 2 tsp garlic purée
2 tbsp tahini
2 tbsp lemon juice
3 tbsp unsweetened natural yogurt
¼ tsp ground cumin
1 tbsp washed and finely chopped flat-leaf parsley leaves
A sprinkling of hot smoked paprika

For the mixed salad
1 tomato, washed and finely chopped
½ red onion, thinly sliced
A few washed lettuce leaves

1   Place the yogurt, oil, vinegar, garlic, pepper, mixed spice or
    allspice and lemon juice in a large non-reactive bowl and mix
    well. Add the chicken slices to the marinade, stir to coat,
    cover and marinate in the fridge for at least 30 minutes (or
    overnight).
2   Preheat the oven to 180°C/350°F/Gas 4.
3   Spread out the chicken on a lined baking tray and bake in the
    oven for 15–20 minutes, until the chicken is cooked through.
    The juices should run clear when a piece is cut in half.
4   To make the tahini sauce, combine the garlic and tahini in a
    bowl, then whisk in the lemon juice and yogurt to form a
    creamy sauce. Stir in the cumin and parsley, then spoon into
    a bowl and sprinkle with the paprika.
5   Cut a pitta bread down the centre to create a pocket and fill
    with the chicken, tomato, onion and lettuce. Top with the
    tahini sauce and serve.

Chicken Chow Mein

Chow mein is a stir-fried noodle dish from America, with Chinese influences. It's a useful way to use up vegetable odds and ends to make a wonderfully fragrantly spiced dish.

For thousands of years, herbs and spices have been used to restore balance in the body. And that is how Chinese five-spice powder came to be. The most common ingredients in Chinese five-spice powder are star anise, fennel seeds, Szechuan peppercorns, whole cloves and cinnamon, though the blend can differ depending which brand you choose.

SERVES 4

150g dried medium egg noodles
1 tsp toasted sesame oil
300g chicken breast fillets, sliced into 5–6cm long strips
2 tbsp low-sodium (low-salt) soy sauce
1 tsp Chinese five-spice powder
1 tbsp cornflour
1 tbsp sunflower oil
1 tbsp peeled and grated root ginger or ginger paste
150g shop-bought fresh vegetable stir-fry mix
2 spring onions, trimmed, washed and thinly sliced
   lengthways
¼ tsp freshly ground black pepper
1 tsp chilli sauce (optional)

1   Cook the noodles in a saucepan of boiling water for 2–3
    minutes, until al dente (firm to the bite), or according to
    instructions on the packet. Drain, then rinse under cold
    running water and drain again. Drizzle with the sesame oil
    and toss through to prevent the noodles from sticking to
    each other.

2   Put the chicken strips in a bowl and season with the soy
    sauce and five-spice powder. Mix well, then lightly dust the
    chicken strips with the cornflour.

3   Heat half the sunflower oil in a large frying pan or a wok over
    a medium-high heat. Tip in the chicken and stir-fry for 7–10
    minutes, or until the chicken is golden brown and cooked
    through. Remove the chicken from the pan and set aside.

4   Heat the remaining ½ tablespoon of oil in the same pan
    (wiped clean with kitchen paper) and tip in the ginger. Mix
    for a minute, then tip in the stir-fry mix. Return the chicken
    to the pan and cook for a further 2 minutes before adding the
    spring onions and stir-frying for 30 seconds. Stir in the
    cooked noodles and add the black pepper. Serve with the
    chilli sauce, if using.

Peri Peri-style Chicken

Traditionally, peri peri is an African sauce made from very hot chillies known as bird's eye chillies, combined with garlic, onion and lemon. Read the label to know what the chilli sauce contains when purchasing a bottle.

Try serving this baked chicken dish with the Portuguese Salad on page 87.

SERVES 4

6 garlic cloves, crushed, or 6 tsp garlic purée

2 tbsp extra virgin olive oil

2 tbsp sherry vinegar or red wine vinegar

1 tbsp sweet smoked paprika

4 tbsp peri peri sauce, Encona hot sauce or your favourite chilli sauce

Juice of 1 lemon

½ tsp freshly ground black pepper

4 skinless and boneless chicken breasts, cut into bite-sized pieces

1 Combine the garlic, olive oil, sherry or red wine vinegar, paprika, peri peri sauce, lemon juice and black pepper in a bowl. Add the chicken, cover and marinate in the fridge for minimum 30 minutes (or overnight).

2 Preheat the oven to 180°C/350°F/Gas 4 and line a baking tray with greaseproof paper.

3 Put the marinated chicken pieces on the lined baking tray and bake in the oven for 30–40 minutes, until the chicken is white on the inside and cooked through.

Lemon Chicken

Packed with vitamin C, lemons are known to help aid the immune system.

Boneless and skinless chicken is low in fat and high in protein so it's good to have in the freezer for simple dishes like this one.

Serve this chicken dish with the Green Salad with Vinaigrette on page 92.

SERVES 2

Grated zest and juice of 1 unwaxed lemon
1 onion, roughly chopped
2 garlic cloves, crushed, or 2 tsp garlic purée
1 tbsp runny honey
Pinch of sea salt (optional)
¼ tsp freshly ground black or white pepper
4 skinless and boneless chicken thighs
A few washed and chopped flat-leaf or curly-leaf
    parsley leaves

1   Place the lemon zest in an ovenproof dish that's large enough
    to hold the chicken pieces. Squeeze the juice of the lemon
    into the dish and discard any pips. Add the onion, garlic,
    honey, salt, if using, and pepper to the dish and mix the
    ingredients well.
2   Using a sharp knife, cut a few deep slashes in the chicken
    thighs, then add the chicken pieces to the dish. Using washed
    hands, work the lemon and onion marinade into the chicken.
    Cover the dish with cling film and put in the fridge to
    marinate for minimum 30 minutes (or overnight).
3   Preheat the oven to 180°C/350°F/Gas 4.
4   Remove the cling film and bake the chicken in the oven for
    35–40 minutes until cooked through, turning the chicken
    pieces from time to time until they are nicely browned all
    over.

Tarka Dal

Tarka dal is an Indian lentil dish made from red lentils, which are rich in soluble and insoluble fibre. Both types of fibre are used for carrying away cholesterol from the heart and removing it from the body. Red lentils are also a great source of magnesium, assisting in relaxing the muscular walls of blood vessels and thereby naturally lowering blood pressure. If you want to make your own panch phoran, see the box opposite.

Serve this dal warm, with wholemeal pitta breads or rice.

SERVES 4

200g red lentils (masoor dal), rinsed and drained
¼ tsp ground turmeric
2 tbsp extra virgin olive oil or unsalted butter
Pinch of asafoetida (optional)
¼ tsp East Indian five-spice mixture (panch phoran)
1 small onion or 2–3 shallots, thinly sliced
1 green chilli, finely chopped
1 tomato, washed and finely chopped

1   Place the rinsed lentils in a saucepan with 400ml boiling water and the turmeric and simmer gently for 25–30 minutes, or until the lentils are tender.
2   Heat the oil or butter in a heavy-based frying pan over a medium heat. Tip in the asafoetida, if using. When it crackles, add the panch phoran and stir for a few seconds, allowing the seeds to crackle. Tip in the onion or shallots and fry for 5 minutes until softened and lightly browned, then stir in the chilli and tomato. Stir the spice mixture into the lentils and cook for a further 2 minutes. Remove from the heat and serve.

EAST INDIAN FIVE-SPICE MIXTURE (PANCH PHORAN)

Combine the following spices and store in an airtight container: ½ tsp fenugreek seeds, 1 tsp cumin seeds, 1 tsp fennel seeds, 1 tsp brown mustard seeds, 1 tsp nigella seeds.

Sausage Casserole

Red peppers not only add vibrant colour to a dish but also are one of the best sources of vitamin C, which is crucial for a healthy immune system. You can use other herbs such as thyme and tarragon to boost the flavour of this casserole, if you wish.

SERVES 4

2 tbsp extra virgin olive oil

2 red onions, thickly sliced

8 chicken, pork or vegetarian sausages

3–4 garlic cloves, finely chopped

2 rosemary sprigs, washed

400g tin cherry tomatoes or chopped tomatoes

1 low-sodium or low-salt stock cube

2 red, yellow or orange peppers, deseeded and roughly chopped

1 tbsp runny honey

1 tbsp Dijon mustard

¼ tsp freshly ground black pepper

1 tbsp Worcestershire sauce (optional)

1 Heat the oil in a shallow dish or pan over a medium heat. Add the onions and sausages and fry for 5–7 minutes, stirring regularly, until the onions are softened and the sausages are browned all over. Stir in the garlic and rosemary and cook for 1 minute, then add the tomatoes and crumble in the stock cube. Stir well and bring to the boil, then reduce the heat to low and stir in the peppers. Simmer, uncovered, for 20 minutes, stirring occasionally.

2 Stir in the honey, mustard, black pepper and Worcestershire sauce, if using. Cover and cook for a further 5 minutes until the sausages are fully cooked through. Remove the rosemary sprigs before serving. Any leftovers can be frozen for up to 3 months.

Wholewheat Macaroni Cheese

This indulgent once-in-a-while treat contains onion, which adds an extra flavour dimension. Onions are nutrient rich and may help reduce heart disease risk factors such as high blood pressure.

You can replace the wholewheat macaroni with any other wholewheat pasta such as penne or fusilli.

Try serving this with the Green Salad with Vinaigrette on page 92.

SERVES 2

140g wholewheat macaroni
1 tbsp unsalted butter
1 onion, finely chopped
60ml semi-skimmed milk
500ml chicken or vegetable stock (can be made from a low-sodium or low-salt stock cube)
60g Cheddar cheese, grated
A few flat-leaf parsley leaves, washed and chopped
¼ tsp freshly ground black pepper

1 Preheat the oven to 180°C/350°F/Gas 4.
2 Cook the macaroni in fresh boiling water according to the instructions on the packet, then drain, rinse, and put the macaroni into an ovenproof casserole dish.
3 Melt the butter in a large saucepan over a medium heat, add the onion and cook for 4–5 minutes until softened, then add the milk and stock and cook for 3–4 minutes, stirring from time to time until slightly thickened. Pour the mixture over the macaroni, then scatter over the cheese.
4 Bake in the oven for 10 minutes, until golden brown on top. Remove from the oven and sprinkle over the parsley and the black pepper.

Lebanese-style Chicken Wraps

These wraps pack a zesty punch with plenty of spice.

Allspice is a spice made from the dried berries of the allspice tree. The spices resemble peppercorns and the warming flavour notes are reminiscent of cinnamon, cloves, nutmeg and pepper. It's used in Caribbean, South American and Middle Eastern cuisines.

SERVES 2

2 skinless and boneless chicken breasts, cut into 5cm-thick pieces, or 250g quorn pieces

125g Greek-style yogurt

Grated zest of ½ unwaxed lemon and 1½ tbsp lemon juice

½ tsp ground allspice

Generous pinch of white pepper

1 tsp extra virgin olive oil

1 tsp runny honey

2 garlic cloves, crushed, or 2 tsp garlic purée

Pinch of sea salt

A few flat-leaf parsley leaves, washed and finely chopped

2 tomatoes, finely chopped

¼ cucumber, washed and chopped or sliced

2 wholewheat wraps

Washed mixed salad leaves

1   In a bowl that's large enough to hold the chicken, mix half the yogurt with the lemon zest, 1 tablespoon of the lemon juice, and the allspice, white pepper, olive oil, honey, garlic and salt. Add the chicken, stir to coat, then cover and marinate in the fridge for a minimum of 1 hour (or overnight).

2   Preheat the oven to 180°C/350°F/Gas 4.

3 Spread the marinated chicken out evenly on a lined baking tray and bake in the oven for 30 minutes, until the chicken is white on the outside and cooked through. You can finish off the chicken under the grill for about 4 minutes until lightly browned, if you wish.

4 Spread the rest of the yogurt over the wraps and fill with the cooked chicken, parsley, tomatoes and cucumber. Drizzle over the remaining ½ tablespoon of the lemon juice and roll up.

5 Put the wraps on a heated griddle or frying pan and warm for 30 seconds each side to lightly toast, then serve with the mixed salad leaves.

Tandoori Chicken

This delicious dish works well with a green salad to boost the greenery and vegetable content. Try serving it with Minted Yogurt Dip (page 130) and Kidney Bean Curry (page 50), too, and dressing the tomatoes with the Indian Salad Dressing on page 125.

SERVES 2

4 skinless chicken drumsticks or 4 skinless and boneless
  chicken thighs
1 tbsp tandoori spice blend
2 garlic cloves, crushed, or 2 tsp garlic purée
1 tbsp tomato purée
1 tbsp lemon juice
75g unsweetened natural yogurt
¼ tsp freshly ground black pepper
1 lemon, cut into wedges
2 tomatoes, washed and chopped

1   Make deep slashes all over the chicken pieces. Combine all
    the rest of the ingredients in a bowl, except the lemon
    wedges and tomatoes, then add the chicken and coat with
    the mixture. If you have time, cover and leave in the fridge to
    marinate for minimum 1 hour (or overnight).
2   Preheat the oven to 190°C/375°F/Gas 5.
3   Transfer the marinated chicken to an ovenproof dish and
    bake in the oven for 35 minutes, until thoroughly cooked and
    slightly charred (bone-in chicken pieces will take longer to
    cook than skinless, boneless chicken).
4   Serve with the lemon wedges and the chopped tomatoes.

Jerk-style Jambalaya

Cajun seasoning is a versatile blend of herbs and piquant spices that can be found in most supermarkets (do remember that shop-bought blends may contain salt). It's great for jazzing up plain yogurt, adding to a marinade or sprinkling on vegetables before roasting.

This dish has lean chicken, which is high in protein and offers an easy way to boost heart health and help lower blood pressure. To add more fibre to this recipe, replace the white rice with brown.

SERVES 2

2 tbsp extra virgin olive oil

2 skinless and boneless chicken breasts, cut into bite-sized pieces

1 onion, finely chopped

1 red pepper, deseeded and thinly sliced

2–4 garlic cloves, crushed, or 2 tsp garlic purée

1½ tbsp Cajun seasoning

2 tsp ground cumin

1 tsp smoked paprika

250g white long-grain rice, such as basmati, washed

200g tinned chopped tomatoes

500ml chicken stock (can be made from a low-sodium or low-salt stock cube)

1   Heat half the olive oil in a large frying pan (with a lid) over a medium heat, add the chicken and sauté for 8–10 minutes until golden. Remove and set aside.

2   Tip the onion into the pan and cook for 3–4 minutes until softened, then add the red pepper, garlic and the Cajun seasoning, cumin and paprika and cook for a further 5 minutes. Return the chicken to the pan and mix, then add the rice and stir to combine. Add the tomatoes and the chicken stock, cover and simmer for 10–12 minutes until the rice is tender. Serve.

Bhuna Chicken

Bhuna is a type of medium-spiced dry Indian dish made from roasted spices. This simple dry curry uses a variety of spices which add to the flavour of the chicken without adding the excess salt and oil that's often used in curries that have more sauce.

Serve with wholemeal pitta breads.

SERVES 4

3 tbsp sunflower or rapeseed oil
4 garlic cloves, finely chopped
1 green chilli, finely chopped
1 tsp peeled and grated root ginger or ginger paste
2 onions, finely chopped
1 tsp ground turmeric
2 tsp medium chilli powder
2 tsp ground cumin
2 tsp ground coriander
¼ tsp garam masala
6 skinless and boneless chicken thighs, cut into 2.5cm pieces
2 tsp tomato purée
1 tsp lemon juice
A few washed and chopped coriander leaves

1 Heat the oil in a large, deep frying pan or wok over a medium heat, add the garlic, green chilli and ginger and cook for a minute, then add the onions. Stir and cook for 3–4 minutes until softened and golden brown, then add the turmeric, chilli powder, ground cumin, ground coriander and garam masala. Stir and cook for about a minute.

2   Add the chicken and stir to coat the pieces in the mixture, then sauté until the chicken is cooked on the outside. Mix in the tomato purée, then pour in about 120ml water and mix again. Reduce the heat, cover and cook for about 10 minutes until the mixture becomes nice and thick and the chicken is tender and cooked through.

3   Stir in the lemon juice to add a little zing, and garnish with the coriander leaves.

4   The dish can be frozen (without the coriander) for up to 3 months. Defrost it thoroughly before reheating and eating.

Chicken Chasseur

Chicken Chasseur is a classic dish that never goes out of favour. It combines mushrooms and chicken in a tomato sauce, making it an accessible autumn combination.

Bacon goes through a curing process where it is soaked in salt and nitrates, so it should be consumed in small quantities and not on a regular basis. If you prefer, you could remove the bacon from this recipe.

Serve with wholegrain rice.

SERVES 2

1 tbsp extra virgin olive oil
4 rashers of streaky bacon, cut into large pieces
2 skinless and boneless chicken breasts, cut into 2.5cm pieces
2 garlic cloves, finely chopped
100g button mushrooms, wiped clean
200g tinned chopped tomatoes
½ vegetable or chicken stock cube (use a low-sodium or low-salt stock cube)
¼ tsp ground white or black pepper
Handful of flat-leaf parsley leaves, washed and chopped

1   Heat the oil in a shallow saucepan over a medium heat, add the bacon and let it sizzle for about 2 minutes until it starts to brown. Add the chicken and fry for 3–4 minutes until it has turned white on the outside. Add the garlic and mushrooms and continue to stir-fry for a few minutes until well combined. Tip in the tomatoes and stir, then crumble in the half stock cube and mix well. Add 125ml water and let everything bubble for 10 minutes, then stir through the pepper and parsley. Remove from the heat and serve.
2   The dish can be frozen for up to 3 months (without the parsley). Defrost it thoroughly before reheating.

Tagliatelle with Chicken and Mushrooms

Creamy, garlicky sauce combined with lean chicken and mushrooms creates a comforting meal in minutes. The fresh garlic can help boost heart health by lowering cholesterol levels. Garlic bulbs keep best when stored in a cool, dry place.

Serve this pasta dish with the Green Salad with Vinaigrette on page 92.

SERVES 4

2 tbsp extra virgin olive oil
2 skinless and boneless chicken breasts, cut into thin pieces
300g tagliatelle
1 onion, thinly sliced
4 garlic cloves, finely chopped
12 mushrooms, wiped clean and thickly sliced
Pinch of chilli flakes (optional)
¼ tsp freshly ground black pepper
2 tbsp single cream, crème fraîche or soured cream
A few washed and roughly chopped flat-leaf parsley leaves, to serve

1   Heat half the oil in a large non-stick frying pan or saucepan over a medium heat, add the chicken and fry for 3–4 minutes on each side until cooked through. Transfer to a plate and set aside.

2   Cook the tagliatelle in fresh boiling water until it is tender but still al dente (firm to the bite). This should take about 10 minutes. Drain the pasta in a colander and run under a cold tap.

3   Heat the remaining oil in the frying pan or saucepan, add the onion and fry for 5 minutes, then tip in the garlic and fry for another minute. Add the mushrooms and stir-fry for a further 4 minutes. Mix in the chilli flakes, if using, and the black pepper, then return the chicken to the pan and cook for 2 minutes more. Stir in the single cream, crème fraîche or soured cream, then add the pasta to the sauce and mix well.

3   Serve immediately, garnished with the parsley.

One-pot Chicken with Parsnips, Honey and Mustard

Parsnips are high in soluble and insoluble fibre, and are a great source of vitamin C. As with so many slow-cooked dishes, this one-pot chicken dish tastes more flavoursome the next day, when the ingredients have had the chance to meld and blend. Serve with mashed potato or green vegetables.

SERVES 4-6

3 tbsp extra virgin olive oil

12 skinless and boneless chicken thighs

2 onions, finely chopped

600g parsnips (about 3 or 4), peeled or scrubbed, washed and roughly chopped

3 garlic cloves, finely chopped

1 tbsp plain flour

3 tbsp Dijon mustard

½ tsp freshly ground black pepper

¼ tsp ground turmeric

1 tbsp runny honey

750ml hot chicken or vegetable stock (can be made from 2 low-sodium or low-salt stock cubes)

4–5 sprigs of thyme or rosemary, washed

Handful of flat-leaf parsley, washed and chopped, to serve

1   Preheat the oven to 170°C/340°F/Gas 3.
2   Heat 2 tablespoons of the olive oil in a large heavy-based casserole over a medium-high heat, add the chicken and brown on both sides (in batches to avoid overcrowding the pan). Add a little more oil if needed. Remove from the pan and set aside.

3 Add the remaining tablespoon of oil to the casserole, add the onions and fry for 5 minutes until softened, then add the parsnips and fry for 5 minutes until golden in places. Stir in the garlic and fry for 1 minute, then stir in the flour to coat the vegetables. Add the mustard, black pepper, turmeric and honey, return the chicken to the pan with any resting juices and pour in the hot stock to cover the chicken. Tuck in the sprigs of thyme or rosemary, bring to a simmer, then cover with a lid, transfer to the oven and bake for 1½ hours. Check the liquid level halfway through the cooking time and add a little water if it looks dry. When ready to serve, remove from the oven and leave to rest with the lid on for 10 minutes.

4 Stir through the parsley and serve.

5 This dish freezes brilliantly. Freeze it in an airtight container (without the parsley) for up to 3 months. Defrost thoroughly before reheating.

Pasta Ratatouille Bake

Make this recipe during the summer months when tomatoes, courgettes and green beans are at their seasonal best and cheapest.

Courgettes are high in water and fibre and can promote healthy digestion, and the skin contains high levels of antioxidants – beneficial plant compounds that help protect your body from damage by free radicals.

Serve this bake warm, with the Iceberg Salad on page 86.

SERVES 4

200g wholewheat macaroni or penne (or any favourite pasta shape)

1 tbsp extra virgin olive oil

2 medium onions, finely chopped

3–4 garlic cloves, crushed, or 2 tsp garlic purée

1 tsp dried oregano

4 courgettes, washed and thinly sliced

200g frozen green beans, tinned green beans, or fresh green beans (if fresh, wash them then top and tail them)

400g tin chopped tomatoes

125ml vegetable or chicken stock (can be made from a low-sodium or low-salt stock cube)

¼ tsp freshly ground black pepper

A few chilli flakes (optional)

25g vegetarian hard cheese or Cheddar cheese, grated

A few basil leaves, washed and chopped

1. Preheat the oven to 180°C/350°F/Gas 4.
2. Cook the pasta in fresh boiling water according to the instructions on the packet, then drain and run under a cold tap. This prevents the pasta from sticking together.
3. Heat the oil in a large saucepan over a medium heat, add the onions and garlic and cook for 5–7 minutes until softened and golden. Stir in the dried oregano, then tip in the courgettes and green beans and sauté for 4–5 minutes. Mix in the tomatoes and cook for another 2 minutes to combine the mixture. Pour in the stock and simmer for 5 minutes.
4. Combine the pasta and the vegetables and season with the black pepper and chilli flakes, if using. Transfer to a baking dish, sprinkle the grated cheese on top, and bake in the oven for 25 minutes until bubbling.
5. Remove from the oven, scatter the basil leaves on top, and return to the oven for another 5 minutes, then remove from the oven and serve.
6. This dish can be frozen on the day of cooking (without the basil leaves) for up to 3 months. Defrost thoroughly before reheating.

Lamb Stew

Barley can help encourage feelings of fullness because of its high fibre content and its nutrients include selenium, a powerful antioxidant that may protect against heart disease and boosts the immune system. Vitamin C-packed celery can assist in reducing inflammation and supports digestion. This stew uses lean lamb which is rich in iron.

Serve with some crusty wholemeal bread and Green Beans with Lemon and Pepper Dressing on page 110.

SERVES 4

125g floury potatoes

2 tbsp extra virgin olive oil or rapeseed oil

200g lean lamb leg (trimmed of fat), cut into chunks

1 bay leaf

1 onion, finely chopped

2 garlic cloves, finely chopped

1 carrot, peeled and cut into thin discs

6–8 mushrooms, wiped clean and thinly sliced

2 celery sticks, washed and cut into pieces

3 tbsp pearl barley

500ml lamb or vegetable stock (can be made from a low-sodium or low-salt stock cube)

¼ tsp freshly ground black pepper

¼ tsp dried thyme

1   Parboil the potatoes for 6–8 minutes and drain. Leave to cool, then peel and cut into cubes.

2   Heat the oil in a saucepan over a medium heat, add the lamb and fry in batches until browned. Remove with a slotted spoon and set aside.

3   Add the bay leaf, onion, garlic, carrot, mushrooms and celery to the same pan and fry for 5–7 minutes until softened, then add the browned lamb, parboiled potatoes, barley and stock to the pan. Season with the black pepper and thyme, cover with a lid and simmer over a low heat for 1 hour until the lamb is tender. Alternatively, brown the meat and soften the vegetables in the saucepan on the hob, then transfer to an ovenproof dish, add the barley, stock and seasoning and bake, covered, for 30 minutes in an oven set at 180°C/350°F/Gas 4. Serve hot.

Desserts

While we don't really need a reason to eat desserts, eating them doesn't mean that you have little or no self-control. It only means that you have a good sense of what you want and that you have what it takes to honour these cravings. You wouldn't eat an entire birthday cake alone, just possibly take a slice and share the rest. More often than not, just a few bites of something sweet should prove to be enough to satisfy the strongest cravings. Whatever dessert you make, always eat in moderation, and to enjoy your sweet things and also stay healthy, make portion control a regular practice.

If you have the baking bug, there's no reason not to switch to making your bakes and sweet treats healthier by swapping plain flour for wholemeal and using unsaturated oil such as sunflower oil in cakes instead of butter. Spices can amp up the flavour without the excessive use of sugar, which can be reduced when mixing batters.

Most citrus fruits are a great source of vitamin C and a small piece of dark chocolate provides antioxidants that can help protect against free radicals.

Apple and Ginger Tart Tatin

The combination of apple and ginger makes this 'upside down' tart a flavoursome showstopper.

Apples are a good source of fibre and vitamin C and work well with cinnamon. Use vanilla extract if you can, not essence: vanilla 'essence' is a manufactured liquid that tastes a bit like vanilla, but contains little or no real vanillin – a molecule found in vanilla beans.

Serve this tart warm, with ice cream.

SERVES 6

15g unsalted butter, plus extra for greasing
20g caster sugar
1 tsp runny honey
¼ tsp ground cinnamon
1 tsp vanilla extract
3–4 eating apples, peeled, cored and quartered
2 balls of stem ginger, chopped
375g ready-rolled all-butter puff or shortcrust pastry

1 Preheat the oven to 180°C/350°F/Gas 4. Grease the base of a 20cm round ovenproof pie dish with butter and line the base and sides with baking parchment or greaseproof paper.

2 Put the sugar and 1 teaspoon of water into a medium non-stick pan, place over a medium heat and swirl the pan gently without stirring until the sugar has dissolved and turned dark golden brown. Stir in the butter, honey, cinnamon and vanilla and simmer for 3–4 minutes until it looks like syrup. Add the apples, turning them in the syrup to coat. Remove from the heat.

3 Pour the syrup from the pan into the pie dish, then arrange the apples in the dish, overlapping slightly, and working in a circular formation from the outside first. Scatter the ginger pieces between the apple quarters.

4 Unroll the pastry, then cut out a circle a little larger than the dish. Lay the pastry over the apples and tuck down the edges into the dish around the filling. Bake in the oven for 40–50 minutes, or until the pastry is cooked and golden.

5 Remove from the oven, leave to cool in the dish for 10 minutes, then turn out carefully onto a serving plate.

Cherries with Vanilla Ricotta and Toasted Almonds

Although high in fat, almonds are a good source of fibre and protein and contain nutrients that can help protect the heart. Compared to other cheeses, ricotta cheese contains less salt and fat. The vitamin C-rich cherries add colour to this dessert.

SERVES 2

2 tbsp ricotta cheese
2 tsp icing sugar
¼ tsp vanilla extract
180ml double cream
12 frozen pitted cherries, sliced in half and defrosted
1 tbsp toasted slivered almonds

1 Combine the ricotta cheese in a bowl with the icing sugar and whip until smooth, then fold in the vanilla.
2 Whisk the cream in a bowl until stiff peaks form, then fold the cream into the ricotta mixture.
3 Put the cherries at the base of each serving dish and top with the ricotta mixture, followed by the almonds, and serve.

Leftover Stollen Pudding

This warming dessert is a great way to use up any leftover stollen cake. This could be a breakfast treat if eaten only once in a while.

No extra sugar has been added to this mix, so most of the sweetness comes from the sultanas and marzipan in the stollen.

SERVES 2

200g stollen cake, cut into 3cm cubes
150ml semi skimmed or plant milk
1 medium free-range egg, beaten
A pinch of nutmeg
A pinch of cinnamon
3 tbsp granola
Single cream, to serve

1 Preheat the oven to 180°C/350°F/Gas 4.
2 Put the stollen cubes into an ovenproof serving dish.
3 In a jug or bowl, mix the milk, egg, nutmeg and cinnamon together and pour over the stollen. Scatter the granola evenly over the dish. Bake in the oven for 30–40 minutes, until golden on top. Serve with single cream.

Mango Dessert

Natural yogurt contains health-boosting bacteria that can help the body fight off infections. Also known as live or probiotic yogurt, it encourages the body to produce anti-viral agents. If you can get hold of fresh mango for this dish, it's even better than tinned as the fruit is an excellent source of beta-carotene, an antioxidant that the body converts to vitamin A.

The yogurt is strained for several hours or overnight to remove most of the water.

SERVES 2

150g unsweetened natural yogurt or bio yogurt

4 tbsp mango pulp or 1 x 450g tin mango slices in juice, drained

2 tbsp whipped cream or unsweetened squirty cream

1   Put the yogurt in a muslin cloth or a nylon sieve. Tie the ends of the muslin cloth together and attach it to a fork or a knife and suspend the whole thing over a bowl to collect the water that drips out. If using a sieve, cover the sieve and suspend the sieve over the bowl. The sieve needs to be covered so that no other aromas or flavours from foods already in the fridge are picked up by the yogurt. Put the bowl in the fridge for about 8 hours or overnight.

2   Put the strained yogurt into a clean bowl and discard the water in the bowl.

3   If you're using a tin of mango, purée the slices in a blender or food processor and pass through a nylon sieve into a bowl, extracting as much of the pulp as possible, which you will use to make the dessert. Discard the fibrous material left in the sieve.

4   Whisk the strained yogurt with the mango pulp until the mixture stiffens, then fold in the whipped or squirty cream. Serve chilled, in two small bowls or ramekins.

Baked Apple with Raisins

Apples contain vitamin C which helps protect against colds and flu, and the soluble fibre contained in the skin can help support good digestion.

Serve this baked apple warm, with a dollop of custard or single cream.

SERVES 1

1 cooking apple
1 tsp unsalted butter
25g raisins
1 tsp light brown sugar

1 Preheat the oven to 200°C/400°F/Gas 6.
2 Using a sharp knife, carefully core the apple to create a cavity large enough to accommodate the raisins (or use an apple corer). Score around the middle with the knife, then place the apple in an ovenproof dish.
3 Mix the butter, raisins and brown sugar together and stuff the mixture into the apple. Place in the middle of the oven and bake for about 30 minutes, or until soft.
4 Remove from the oven and serve.

Rhubarb Crumble

Rhubarb, a sharp and vitamin C-loaded vegetable that we often sweeten and cook like a fruit, contains anti-bacterial properties that assist the body in fighting off infections. Using wholemeal flour instead of white plain flour for this recipe adds fibre which is good for the gut.

Serve warm, with custard.

SERVES 4

3–4 sticks of rhubarb, trimmed and washed
4 tbsp caster sugar
1 tsp ground ginger
110g unsalted butter, softened
200g wholemeal flour
50g demerara or light brown sugar

1 Preheat the oven to 180°C/350°F/Gas 4.
2 Cut the rhubarb into 7.5cm sticks, spread out on an oven tray and sprinkle with 2 tablespoons of water and the caster sugar. Roast in the oven for 10 minutes. Remove from the oven, sprinkle over the ginger and mix well. Fill a 23cm ovenproof dish (about 4cm deep) with the rhubarb.
3 Rub the butter into the flour and sugar in a bowl to make the crumble topping. Sprinkle the crumble evenly over the rhubarb and bake in the oven for 35–45 minutes, or until the crumble topping is crisp and golden brown and the rhubarb filling has softened and is bubbling.
4 Remove from the oven and allow to cool slightly before serving. It will keep in the fridge for a few days and can be frozen for up to 4 months.

Mixed Berry Sponge Pudding

Berries are rich in antioxidants, which may help protect your cells from free-radical damage. This semi-steamed pudding is lovely on a cold winter's day, or for a special occasion. Serve warm, with custard or ice cream.

SERVES 4

125g unsalted butter, softened, plus 1 tbsp melted
1 tsp vanilla extract
115g caster sugar, plus 1 tbsp for sprinkling
2 medium free-range eggs
165g self-raising flour, sifted
60ml semi-skimmed milk
200g mixed berries, fresh or thawed if frozen (such as blackberries, blueberries or blackcurrants)

1 Preheat the oven to 180°C/350°F/Gas 4. Line the base and sides of a 20cm square cake tin (don't use a springform tin for this recipe) with baking parchment or greaseproof paper and pour in the tablespoon of melted butter.

2 Cream the softened butter, vanilla extract and sugar in a bowl using an electric mixer until pale and fluffy. Add the eggs one at a time, beating well after each addition, then gently fold in the flour a little at a time, alternating with the milk.

3 Scatter the berries in the cake tin on top of the melted butter and sprinkle with the tablespoon of caster sugar, then spoon the batter over the berries.

4 Get a large roasting tin (larger than the cake tin) and place the cake tin in the roasting tin. Carefully and slowly pour enough hot water into the roasting tin to come halfway up the side of the baking tin. Cover the roasting tin with foil, sealing it tightly around the edges, then bake in the middle of the oven for 35–40 minutes, or until the pudding springs back when touched.

5 Remove from the oven and take the cake tin out of the roasting tin. Leave on a rack to cool, then turn it out. The sponge will keep, covered, in the fridge for up to 3–4 days.

Lemon Sponge Cake

Cakes made with oil tend to be lighter and moister than cakes made with butter. Oil is generally comprised of unsaturated fats.

SERVES 16

Unsalted butter, for greasing
Grated zest and juice of 1 large unwaxed lemon
150g caster sugar
160g unsweetened natural yogurt
150ml sunflower or rapeseed oil
270g self-raising flour
2 medium free-range eggs

1. Preheat the oven to 160°C/325°F/Gas 3. Grease the base of a 20cm round or square loose-bottomed cake tin with butter and line with baking parchment or greaseproof paper.

2. Place the lemon zest in a large bowl and add the sugar, yogurt, oil, lemon juice, flour and eggs. Mix everything together with a wooden spoon for 1 minute, then pour the mixture into the lined cake tin. Bake in the middle of the oven for 55 minutes, or until risen and springy when touched.

3. Remove the cake from the oven and leave the cake in its tin on a rack to cool completely before turning it out. Once completely cooled, turn out and slice the lemon sponge into 16 portions.

4. The cake will keep, covered, in the fridge for 6–7 days or can be frozen for up to 3–6 months (defrost thoroughly before eating).

Carrot Muffins

The moment these muffins are removed from the oven, they emanate the delicious aromas of warming spices. Like all foods, muffins should be eaten in moderation.

Carrots are nutritious and are a good source of beta-carotene, a compound that your body changes into vitamin A.

MAKES 10-12 MUFFINS

175ml sunflower oil
75g light brown sugar
1 medium free-range egg
150g carrots, peeled, washed and finely grated
75g plain flour
75g wholemeal flour
1 tsp baking powder
½ tsp bicarbonate of soda
½ tsp ground cinnamon
¼ tsp freshly grated nutmeg

1 Preheat the oven to 180°C/350°F/Gas 4. Place 10–12 paper muffin cases in the holes of a muffin tin.

2 Using an electric mixer, whisk the oil with the sugar in a bowl until light and fluffy. Beat in the egg and add 1 tablespoon of cold water, then stir in the grated carrots.

3 Combine the plain and wholemeal flour, baking powder, bicarbonate of soda, cinnamon and nutmeg in a bowl, then add to the wet ingredients and stir to combine. Spoon the batter evenly into the muffin cases, filling them almost to the top, and bake in the middle of the oven for about 30 minutes, until risen and firm in the middle.

4 Remove from the oven and leave to stand in the tin for 10 minutes, then transfer to a rack to cool. These muffins can be frozen for up to 3 months (defrost thoroughly before eating).

Spiced Chocolate Cake

The inclusion of wholemeal flour makes this cake rich in fibre, while the cinnamon gives it a spicy edge. Cut the cake into squares and serve with a cup of tea or coffee.

SERVES 16

125g wholemeal flour
75g plain flour
1 tsp baking powder
25g unsweetened cocoa powder
1 level tsp ground cinnamon
75g unsalted butter, softened
150g caster sugar
1 tsp vanilla extract
150g unsweetened natural yogurt
150ml sunflower or rapeseed oil
2 medium free-range eggs

1   Preheat the oven to 180°C/350°F/Gas 4. Grease the base and sides of a 20cm loose-bottomed square cake tin and line with baking parchment or greaseproof paper.
2   Sift the flours, baking powder, cocoa powder and cinnamon together in a bowl and set aside.
3   Whisk the butter, sugar, vanilla extract, yogurt and oil together with the eggs using an electric mixer to make a fairly smooth mixture. Tip in the sifted dry ingredients and fold them in gently with a metal spoon until fully combined, then transfer to the lined tin. Place in the centre of the oven and bake in the centre of the oven for 20–25 minutes, until the cake is springy to the touch.
4   Remove from the oven and allow to cool before cutting into squares. The cake can be frozen for up to 3 months.

Marmalade and Fresh Ginger Loaf

Fresh ginger gives this cake zing, and the moist texture that comes from the marmalade makes this a welcome treat.

SERVES 8

120g unsalted butter, softened, plus extra for greasing
80g caster sugar
2 medium free-range eggs, lightly beaten
1 tbsp peeled and grated root ginger or ginger paste
100g wholemeal flour
20g plain flour
1 tsp baking powder
3 tbsp orange marmalade

1 Preheat the oven to 180°C/350°F/Gas 4. Grease the base and sides of a small (450g) loaf tin, and line the base and sides with baking parchment or greaseproof paper.

2 Beat the butter in a bowl with a wooden spoon or electric mixer until creamy. Add the sugar and beat until the mixture lightens in colour and becomes fluffy. Beat in the eggs and the ginger.

3 Combine the flours and baking powder well in a separate bowl, then add to the butter, sugar and egg mixture and fold in, followed by the marmalade. Spoon the mixture into the lined loaf tin and level out the top of the mixture. Bake in the centre of the oven for 40–45 minutes until golden brown and firm to the touch. A cocktail stick inserted into the cake should come out clean.

4 Remove from the oven, allow to cool for 5 minutes, then run a round-bladed knife around the inside of the tin and turn it out onto a wire rack. Leave to cool before slicing.

Christmas Bread and Butter Pudding

This is an easy way to use up festive ingredients that you may have in the store cupboard.

Serve it warm with a drizzle of single cream.

SERVES ABOUT 12

250g bread, a mixture of white and wholemeal works well
200g mixed dried fruit, a mixture of sultanas and currants,
    or 200g mincemeat
50g dark chocolate chips
40g mixed candied peel
½ tsp mixed spice
300ml semi-skimmed milk
1 medium free-range egg, beaten
50g demerara or dark brown sugar
Grated zest of 1 unwaxed lemon
50g unsalted butter, melted, plus extra for greasing
Icing sugar, for dusting

1   Tear the bread into a large mixing bowl and add the dried
    fruit or mincemeat, chocolate chips, mixed candied peel and
    mixed spice. Add the milk and mix with a wooden spoon to
    combine everything and to break up the bread. Add the
    beaten egg, sugar and lemon zest, stir well, then set aside for
    15 minutes to allow the bread to soak up all the flavours.
2   Preheat the oven to 180°C/350°F/Gas 4. Butter the base of a
    20cm non-stick, loose-bottomed square cake tin and line it
    with baking parchment or greaseproof paper.
3   Stir the melted butter into the bread pudding mixture, then
    tip it into the lined tin and level it out. Bake for 1 hour in the
    centre of the oven, or until firm and golden brown. Check the
    pudding halfway through cooking, and if it starts to brown
    too much, cover it with foil and continue to bake.
4   Leave to cool a little in the tin, then turn it out and strip off
    the paper. Dust the pudding with icing sugar and cut into
    squares.

Cranberry Mocktail

Cranberry juice is rich in vitamin C and, combined with warming sage, creates this autumnal mocktail.

SERVES 2
100ml cranberry juice
Juice of 1 orange
6 sage leaves, washed
80ml white grape juice
100ml sparkling water

1 Pour 50ml cranberry juice into two champagne coupes or wine glasses. Divide the orange juice between them, then stir. Add 3 sage leaves and an ice cube or two to each glass, then top up with the grape juice followed by the sparkling water.

ACKNOWLEDGEMENTS

Everyone at Open Age – Iain Cassidy, Jenny Marshall, Russell John, Geoff Brown, Bee Burgess, Tina Lavenu, David Singleton, Herve Bessieres, Richard Ludlow, Maude Chinery, Vie Royal, Angela Sharkey, Paul McGowan, Emma Cohen, Simon Cohen, Dede Tavares, Kalelah Benjamin, Qamile Veliu, Vivienne Mitchell, Caitlin Campbell, Tania d'Alcor, Carolyn English, Lesley Barnes, Teresa Mulligan, Yvonne DSilva, Judah The Lion, Richard Davies, Pat Davies, Albert Buhagiar, Ted Cuming, Ken 'Dalton' Richards, Herbert Jordan, Paul Meade, Peter Onwu.

My mum Kami, Meno Marley, Eva Marley, Isla Marley, Candice Manson, Zac, Tosh Verma, Sharan Verma, Jasmyn Verma, Diya Verma, award-winning journalist Minreet Kaur, Pritpal Kaur and Rajinder Singh The Skipping Sikh, Neena Sohal, Rinku Mitra, Hermina Heder, Hubert Heder, Nureen Glaves, Pedro Carvalho, Indiraa, Rajiv Batra, Taz Virdee, Terry Noad, Debbie Noad, Leon Williams, Callum Wills, Tarek Mrad, Taj Ranger, Layba Nisar, Nafeesa, Nimesh Pattani, Bav Parmar, Aryan Parmar, Nicola Arnold, Jane Coker, Sobia Bi, Rahima Josan, Rama Kaur, Bavjot Kaur, David Thurman, Teresa Thurman, Liliana Sargent, Daniel Sargent, Kapil Lund, Sanjay Suresh, Sharnjeet Bhalla, Geeta Handa London, Catherine Hudson, Daniel Hudson, Shika Patel, Amrit Maan, Ian Barclay, Chandrika Kaviraj, Chip Colquhoun, Professor Trudi Deakin, Jill Franklin, Frances Ma, Janet Sawyer Littlepod Vanilla, Gouri Kubair Holy Lama Spice Drops, Priyesh Patel Cofresh Foods, Girjashanker Vohra, Monica Narula, Monir Ali, Abha Adams, Sean Adams, Shahid Mehdi Real Basmati Rice, Barry Quinn, Robin Dunt, Reg Sanders, Michael Connock, Ian Hewitt, Mika Saha, Elaine Saha, Chloe Marley, John Mwale, Michelle Mwale, Marby Brar, Seb Minhas, Charlie Millar, Julius Asiaw, Alban Echchelh, Amelie Lahouaoui, Victoria Echchelh, Sally King, Ella Aziz, Kay Cotton, Natalie Cotton, Natalie Robertson, Barbara Squires, Alison Whitlock, Jaqui Nainby, Pearly Pih, Yoke Meng, Angela Lee, Ann Tully, Malcolm Smith, Adrian Beale, Dan Ince, Michelle Lewis, Lesley Tucker and OJ Borg.

CONVERSION CHARTS

WEIGHT

Metric	Imperial
25g	1oz
50g	2oz
75g	3oz
100g	4oz
150g	5oz
175g	6oz
200g	7oz
225g	8oz
250g	9oz
300g	10oz
350g	12oz
400g	14oz
450g	1lb

OVEN TEMPERATURES

Celsius	Fahrenheit
110°C	225°F
120°C	250°F
140°C	275°F
150°C	300°F
160°C	325°F
170°C	340°F
180°C	350°F
190°C	375°F
200°C	400°F
220°C	425°F
230°C	450°F
240°C	475°F

LIQUIDS

Metric	Imperial	US cup
5ml	1 tsp	1 tsp
15ml	1 tbsp	1 tbsp
50ml	2fl oz	3 tbsp
60ml	2½fl oz	¼ cup
75ml	3fl oz	⅓ cup
100ml	4fl oz	scant ½ cup
125ml	4½fl oz	½ cup
150ml	5fl oz	⅔ cup
200ml	7fl oz	scant 1 cup
250ml	9fl oz	1 cup
300ml	½ pint	1¼ cups
350ml	12fl oz	1 ½ cups
400ml	¾ pint	1¾ cups
500ml	17fl oz	2 cups
600ml	1 pt	2½ cups

Index

....

overweight 6